Are you ready to have some fun?

Thank you so much for ordering the Pre-K YOUR Way Curriculum Series. I created these activities to support caring parents and teachers like you in creating meaningful learning experience for your children. I hope you enjoy these activities as much as I enjoyed creating them.

Please contact me with any questions or comments that you have while working through the curriculum booklet. I want to hear from **YOU!**

If you enjoy these activities, please write a review on the product that you purchased. All products can be found at:

www.jdeducational.com

Happy Playing, Learning and Growing!

Sincerely,

Jeana Kinne

Copyright@2020 Jeana Kinne/JDEducational

Pre-K YOUR Way Curriculum Series Materials may not be copied or distributed without written permission of JDEducational. Additional curriculum can be purchased at www.jdeducational.com

All rights reserved

ISBN: 9798650660996

- These alphabet activities focus on letter identification and literacy concepts.
- There are five activities related to each letter.
- The first letter activity introduces the shape of the letter.
- The second and third activities use art materials to reinforce the shape of the letter.
- The fourth and fifth activities incorporate literacy and gross motor skills to introduce phonological concepts.

Table of Contents:

Letter	Page #
A	4-7
B	8-11
C	12-15
D	16-19
E	20-23
F	24-27
G	28-31
H	32-35
I	36-40
J	41-43
K	44-46
L	47-49
M	50-55
N	56-60
O	61-64
P	65-69
Q	70-73
R	74-77
S	78-83
T	84-87
U	88-91
V	92-95
W	96-99
X	100-103
Y	104-106
Z	107-110
Review Game	111
Appendix 1 (Clay Recipe)	112
About the Curriculum	113
About the Author	114
Next Steps	115-116

Activity #1: "A"

Materials Needed:
- Paper
- Black Marker, Crayon or Pen
- Glue
- Popsicle Sticks

Instructions:

Step 1: Have an adult draw an "**A**" on a large piece of paper.

Step 2: Encourage the child to glue Popsicle Sticks onto the lines of the letter "**A**" that is on the paper.

Activity #2: Clay "A"

Materials Needed:
- Oven
- Clay Materials (see recipe)

Instructions:

Step 1: The adult and child should make Clay (see recipe in Appendix A) together.

Step 2: Once made, roll the clay out into a long line.

Step 3: Form the clay into the letter "**A**".

Step 4: Bake the clay as described in the recipe.

Activity #3: Clay "A" Decoration

Materials Needed:
- Baked "A" from Activity #2 (see above)
- Watercolors
- Optional: Sequins or glitter and glue

Instructions:

Step 1: Place the clay "**A**" on a baking tray lined with wax paper.

Step 2: Encourage your child to use watercolors and a paintbrush to paint the clay letter. If desired, provide your child with sequins or glitter and glue, allowing them to decorate the letter.

Step 3: Place the project on a shelf overnight to dry.

© JDEducational Curriculum Series: Level 2 Module 1

Activity #4: Apple Prints

Materials Needed:
- ☐ One (1) Red Apple
- ☐ One (1) Green Apple
- ☐ One (1) Yellow Apple
- ☐ Finger Paints (Red, Green and Yellow)
- ☐ One (1) Piece of each of the following colored paper: Red, Yellow and Green
- ☐ One (1) Black Marker
- ☐ One (1) Knife (for adult use only)
- ☐ One (1) Paper Plate

Instructions:

Step 1: The **A**dult should show the child the **a**pples. Explain to the child that **A**pple starts with the letter "**A**".

Step 2: Next, the adult should cut each **a**pple in half.

Step 3: Put some green finger paint in one empty paper plate, red finger paint in one empty paper plate and some yellow finger paint in one empty paper plate.

Step 4: Next, draw the letter **A** on each piece of colored paper.

Step 5: Encourage your child to make apple prints by dipping the **yellow apple** into the **yellow finger paint,** then placing the **a**pple onto the yellow paper with the **A** on it.

Step 6: Repeat Step 5 with the rest of the **a**pples, dipping the **red apple** in **red finger paint**, then placing it on the **Red** paper AND dipping the **green apple** into the **green finger paint**, stamping the **green paper.**

Step 7: Although these are all **a**pples, they are different colors.

Step 8: Can the child name all of the different colors and match them correctly?

Activity #5: Olympic Athlete

Materials Needed:
- ☐ Two (2) piece of colored paper
- ☐ One (1) roll of scotch tape.
- ☐ One (1) timer (cell phone or watch)

Instructions:

Step 1: Tell the child that one of the Olympic sports is running. Today they're going to "train" to become an Olympic Runner **A**thlete.

Step 2: Place two pieces of colored paper on opposite sides of a bedroom or backyard. Make sure to tape the paper down on the ground with scotch tape so it doesn't move.

Step 3: Tell the child you're going to time them to see how fast they can run from one piece of paper to the other piece of paper.

Step 4: On your mark, get set, go! When they start to run, the adult should look at the time. As soon as the child steps on the other piece of paper, stop the clock and see how long it took the child to get there.

Step 5: Repeat Steps 3 through 4 at least four more times. Is your child getting faster? Explain to your child that Olympic **A**thletes train every day to get faster and faster. **A**thlete starts with **A**!

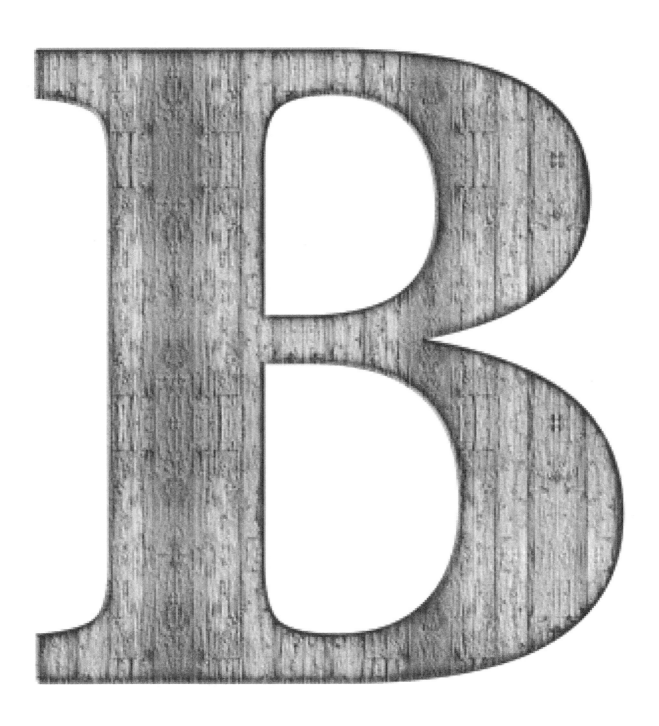

Activity #1: Buttoned Up "B"

Materials Needed:
- ☐ One (1) Piece of Paper
- ☐ Ten (10) to (15) Buttons of various shapes and sizes
- ☐ One (1) Black Marker
- ☐ One (1) Glue Stick

Instructions:

** Caution – Buttons can be a choking hazard if a child places a button in their mouth. Make sure to supervise children during this activity at all times.

- **Step 1:** Draw a **B** on a large piece of blank paper.

- **Step 2:** Encourage your child to glue the **b**lue **b**uttons onto the "**B**".

- **Step 3:** Talk about how the words blue and button starts with "**B**".

Activity #2: Clay "B"

Materials Needed:
- ☐ Oven
- ☐ Clay Materials (see recipe)

Instructions:

- **Step 1:** The Adult and Child should make Clay (see recipe in Appendix A) together.

- **Step 2:** Once made, roll the clay out into a long line.

- **Step 3:** Form the clay into the letter "**B**".

- **Step 4:** Bake the clay as described in the recipe.

© JDEducational Curriculum Series: Level 2 Module 1

Activity #3: Clay "B" Decoration

Materials Needed:
- ☐ Baked "B" from Activity #2 (see above)
- ☐ Watercolors
- ☐ Optional: Sequins or glitter and glue

Instructions:

- **Step 1:** Place the clay "B" on a baking tray lined with wax paper.

- **Step 2:** Encourage your child to use watercolors and a paintbrush to paint the clay letter. If desired, provide your child with sequins or glitter and glue, allowing them to decorate the letter.

- **Step 3:** Place the project on a shelf overnight to dry.

Activity #4: B is for Book

Materials Needed:
- ☐ One (1) Children's Book
- ☐ One (1) Pen
- ☐ One (1) Piece of Blank Paper

Instructions:

- **Step 1:** Sit with your child and allow them to pick out their favorite **b**ook.

- **Step 2:** Have them open up to the first page of the story and show them one letter "**b**" that's in the **b**ook.

- **Step 3:** Help your child read the **b**ook. While you're reading the pages, tell them to look at the letters and point to the letter "**b**" if they see it.

- **Step 4:** Every time your child sees the letter "**b**" and points it out, make a tally mark on a piece of **b**lank paper.

- **Step 5:** When the story is finished, encourage your child to help you count the total number of tally marks from Step 4. How many "**b**'s" were in the story?

Activity #5: Bouncing Ball Run

Materials Needed:
- ☐ One (1) large ball (Basketball, Soccer Ball, Rubber Red Ball)
- ☐ One (1) small ball (Tennis, Baseball, Golf)
- ☐ Outdoor concrete space

Instructions:

- **Step 1:** Allow your child to pick one small ball and one large ball.

- **Step 2:** The adult should show the child how to **bounce** a **ball**.

- **Step 3:** Encourage your child to try and **bounce** the **ball**. Can **b**oth of the **b**alls that they chose **b**ounce?

- **Step 4:** Tell them that "**B**all" and "**B**ounce" start with the letter "**b**"

    - **Option #1:** If you have a **b**asketball hoop, encourage your child to **b**ounce the **b**all then throw it towards the hoop. If you don't have a **b**asketball hoop, tell the child to throw the **b**all into **b**ox or empty **b**in.

    - **Option #2:** Can your child run while **b**ouncing the **b**all?

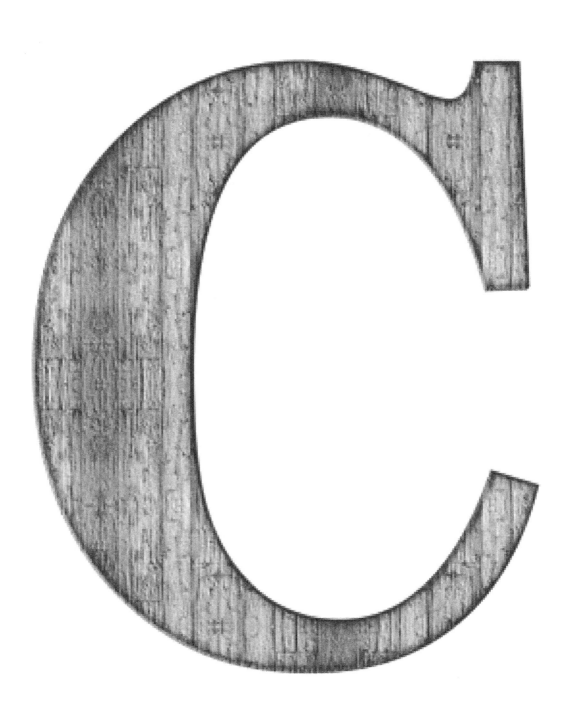

Activity #1: Cotton Ball "C"

Materials Needed:
- ☐ Paper
- ☐ Black Marker, Crayon or Pen
- ☐ Glue
- ☐ Cotton Balls

Instructions:

- **Step 1:** Have an adult draw a "**C**" on a large piece of paper.

- **Step 2:** Encourage the child to glue **C**otton Balls on the letter "**C**" that is on the paper.

Activity #2: Clay "C"

Materials Needed:
- ☐ Oven
- ☐ Clay Materials (see recipe)

Instructions:

- **Step 1:** The adult and **c**hild should make **C**lay (see recipe in Appendix A) together.

- **Step 2:** Once made, roll the **c**lay out into a long line.

- **Step 3:** Form the **c**lay into the letter "**C**".

- **Step 4:** Bake the **c**lay as described in the recipe.

Activity #3: Clay "C" Decoration

Materials Needed:
- ☐ Baked "C" from Activity #2 (see above)
- ☐ Watercolors
- ☐ Optional: Sequins or glitter and glue

Instructions:

- **Step 1:** Place the clay "C" on a baking tray lined with wax paper.

- **Step 2:** Encourage the child to use watercolors and a paintbrush to paint the clay letter. If desired, provide your child with sequins or glitter and glue, allowing them to decorate the letter.

- **Step 3:** Place the project on a shelf overnight to dry.

Activity #4: Celebratory Card

Materials Needed:
- ☐ One (1) Blank Construction Paper (Any color)
- ☐ Crayons or Markers (Any color)
- ☐ One (1) Yellow Highlighter
- ☐ One (1) Pen
- ☐ One (1) Envelope
- ☐ One (1) Stamp
- ☐ Optional: Stickers

Instructions:

- **Step 1:** Ask the child to pick one (or more) person they would like to celebrate today? Tell the child they will make a card for that person.

- **Step 2:** Have your child create a card for that person by decorating a piece of blank construction paper with art materials of your choice.

- **Step 3:** When they have completed the decorations, ask your child what they would like to say in their card. Ask your child what they like best about the person and why the person is special to them. Inside the card, write down what the child says with a yellow highlighter.

- **Step 4:** Next, encourage your child to use a pen to trace the words you wrote in yellow highlighter.

- **Step 5:** When completed, show your child the envelope that you are going to use to send the letter. Fold the letter and show the child where you are going to write the return and send addresses. Allow your child to help place the stamp on the envelope. Do they remember how much a stamp is worth (Activity A3)?

- **Step 6:** Encourage your child to help mail the letter by putting it in the mailbox the next day.

Activity #5: Colored Bubbles

** Note: This is a recipe I used for my preschool classes. You can search the internet for other recipes with variations.

Materials Needed:
- ☐ One and one half (1 1/2) cups of hot water
- ☐ One quarter (¼) cup of light corn syrup
- ☐ One quarter (¼) cup of dish soap
- ☐ One (1) tablespoon of washable paint
- ☐ One (1) plastic cup
- ☐ One (1) bubble Wand
- ☐ One (1) Stamp
- ☐ One (1) Piece of white paper
- ☐ One (1) Box of Crayons
- ☐ One (1) Black marker

Instructions:

- **Step 1:** Mix 1 ½ cups hot water, ¼ cup light corn syrup, ¼ cup dish soap and one tablespoon (or more to preferred color) of washable paint into a plastic cup.

- **Step 2:** Put a bubble wand in the mixture and use as you would to blow regular bubbles!
  - **Optional:** To encourage color recognition, make three or more batches of colored bubbles, each with a different paint color.

- **Step 3:** The adult should ask the child to identify colors of the bubbles.

- **Step 4:** Using a blank piece of paper and black marker, the adult should write the colors the child said in step 3.

- **Step 5:** Have the child trace the color words in step 4 using the corresponding crayon color (trace the word "blue" with a blue crayon).

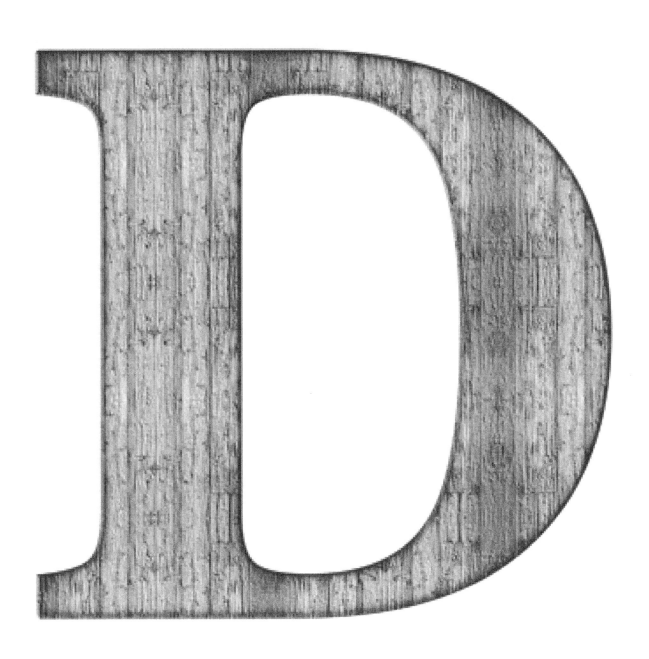

Activity #1: Dotted "D"

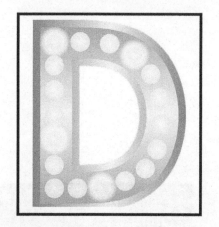

Materials Needed:
- ☐ One (1) Piece of Paper
- ☐ One (1) Set of Watercolor Paint with brush
- ☐ One (1) Black Marker

Instructions:

- **Step 1:** Draw a **D** on a large piece of blank paper.

- **Step 2:** Encourage your child to use the paintbrush, dipped in watercolor paints to make **d**ots on the "**D**".

Activity #2: Clay "D"

Materials Needed:
- ☐ Oven
- ☐ Clay Materials (see recipe)

Instructions:

- **Step 1:** The adult and child should make Clay (see recipe in Appendix A) together.

- **Step 2:** Once made, roll the clay out into a long line.

- **Step 3:** Form the clay into the letter "**D**".

- **Step 4:** Bake the clay as described in the recipe.

Activity #3: Clay "D" Decoration

Materials Needed:
- ☐ Baked "D" from Activity #2 (see above)
- ☐ Watercolors
- ☐ Optional: Sequins or glitter and glue

Instructions:

- **Step 1:** Place the clay "**D**" on a baking tray lined with wax paper.

- **Step 2:** Encourage the child to use watercolors and a paintbrush to paint the clay letter. If desired, provide your child with sequins or glitter and glue, allowing them to decorate the letter.

- **Step 3:** Place the project on a shelf overnight to dry.

Activity #4: D is for Dessert

Materials Needed:
- ☐ Your Favorite Family Dessert Recipe
- ☐ All Ingredients to make the Dessert you chose.
- ☐ All Kitchen Utensils and appliances to make the Dessert you chose.

Instructions:

Step 1: With your child, read the list of materials/ingredients that you need to make your family's favorite **d**essert.

Step 2: Encourage your child to help you find each item in your kitchen.

Step 3: Bring all the items to your kitchen table with the recipe and **d**irections.

Step 4: Allow your child to help you make the **d**essert using the materials on the table.

Step 5: Eat the **d**essert together once it is ready.

Step 6: Are there any ingredients that start with the letter "**D**" in the **d**essert recipe?

Activity #5: Dancing Dinosaurs

Materials Needed:
- ☐ Child Friendly Music
- ☐ An open space for dancing

Instructions:

- **Step 1:** Play some child-friendly music near an open area that's safe for **d**ancing.

- **Step 2:** Every twenty seconds, pause the music and **d**irect your child to freeze.

- **Step 3:** When frozen, tell them to "roar" like a loud **D**inosaur roars.

- **Step 4:** Repeat steps 3 and 4 for as long as you like!

Activity #1: I Hear With my Ear "E"

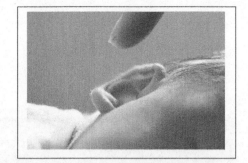

Materials Needed:
- ☐ Magazines/Newspapers
- ☐ Child Safe Scissors
- ☐ Glue Stick
- ☐ Blank Piece of White Paper
- ☐ Black Marker

Instructions:

Step 1: Use a black marker to draw a large "**E**" on a piece of blank white paper.

Step 2: Ask your child to look through appropriate magazines and newspapers to find pictures of items that make **noises and sounds** (we hear with our ears).

Step 3: Encourage your child to cut out the pictures of items that make noise, using child-safe scissors.

Step 4: Explain to the child that we hear **sounds/noises** with our **e**ars! **E**ars start with letter "**E**".

Step 5: Tell them to glue the pictures they cut out onto the piece of paper with the letter "**E**" on it.

Activity #2: Clay "E"

Materials Needed:
- ☐ Oven
- ☐ Clay Materials (see recipe)

Instructions:

Step 1: The adult and child should make Clay (see recipe in Appendix A) together.

Step 2: Once made, roll the clay out into a long rope.

Step 3: Form the clay into the letter "**E**".

Step 4: Bake the clay as described in the recipe.

Activity #3: Clay "E" Decoration

Materials Needed:
- ☐ Baked "E" from Activity #2 (see above)
- ☐ Watercolors
- ☐ Optional: Sequins or glitter and glue

Instructions:

Step 1: Place the clay "**E**" on a baking tray lined with wax paper.

Step 2: Encourage the child to use watercolors and a paintbrush to paint the clay letter. If desired, provide the child with sequins or glitter and glue, allowing them to decorate the letter.

Step 3: Place the project on a shelf overnight to dry.

Activity #4: Eggerific "E"

Materials Needed:
- ☐ One (1) Hardboiled egg
- ☐ One (1) Yellow Highlighter
- ☐ One (1) Pen
- ☐ One (1) Blank Piece of White Paper

Instructions:

Step 1: Have your child hold the hardboiled **e**gg and ask them what it is.

Step 2: Ask them if they know where **e**ggs come from. Use a yellow highlighter to write down what they say on a blank piece of paper. This is a creative story. It's okay if your child uses imagination and creates a story about eggs that may not be true!

Step 3: Encourage your child to use a pen to trace the words you wrote with a pen.

Activity #5: Elephant Tag

Materials Needed:
- ☐ One (1) adult
- ☐ One (1) child
- ☐ Indoor or Outdoor running space

Instructions:

Step 1: Assign tag roles to the participants:

- Person #1: Is the **E**lephant. They try to tag the other person with their trunk.
- Person #2: Runs form the **E**lephant (person #1)

Step 2: Tell your child to put their arms straight out in front of them and clasp their hands together.

That is their trunk. Can they tag/catch the other person by tapping them with their 'trunk'?

Activity #1: Feather Painting

Materials Needed:
- ☐ One (1) Piece of Paper
- ☐ One (1) Finger paint color
- ☐ One (1) Craft Feather
- ☐ One (1) Black Marker

Instructions:

Step 1: Draw an "**F**" on a large piece of blank paper.

Step 2: Encourage the child to dip the end of the craft **f**eather into the **f**inger paint and trace the letter "**F**".

Activity #2: Clay "F"

Materials Needed:
- ☐ Oven
- ☐ Clay Materials (see recipe)

Instructions:

Step 1: The Adult and Child should make Clay (see recipe in Appendix A) together.

Step 2: Once made, roll the clay out into a long line.

Step 3: Form the clay into the letter "**F**".

Step 4: Bake the clay as described in the recipe.

Activity #3: Clay "F" Decoration

Materials Needed:
- ☐ Baked "**F**" from Activity #2 (see above)
- ☐ Watercolors
- ☐ Optional: Sequins or glitter and glue

Instructions:

Step 1: Place the clay "**F**" on a baking tray lined with wax paper.

Step 2: Encourage the child to use watercolors and a paintbrush to paint the clay letter. If desired, provide the child with sequins or glitter and glue, allowing them to decorate the letter.

Step 3: Place the project on a shelf overnight to dry.

Activity #4: F is for Fingers

Materials Needed:
- ☐ Finger-paints
- ☐ One (1) Blank piece of Construction Paper (Any light color)
- ☐ One (1) Black marker
- ☐ One (1) Pen
- ☐ One (1) Lined piece of paper

Instructions:

Step 1: Have your child rub finger-paint all over both of their **hands**.

Step 2: Help them make **handprints** on a piece of construction paper.

Step 3: Tell your child these are their "**Helping Hands**".

Step 4: With the black marker, write "**Helping Hands**" on the top of the construction paper.

Step 5: Have the child count the total number of fingers they have on both of their hands (Answer: 10 fingers)

Step 6: Ask your child to think of **10 ways** (one way for each finger) of how they can use their "**helping hands**" to help others. Write what they say down on a blank piece of lined paper.

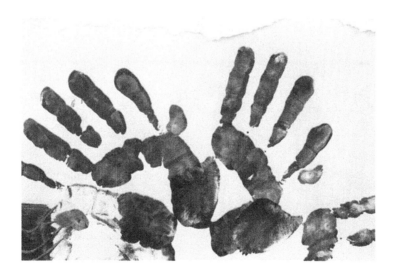

Activity #5: The "Fast" Jump

Materials Needed:
- ☐ A Jump rope
- ☐ An open space for Jumping

Instructions:

Step 1: If there are two adults available, have each adult hold onto one end of the jump rope. If there is one adult available, tie one end of the jump rope onto a tree or fence and the adult hold the other side.

Step 2: Tell your child they need to jump **over** the jump rope as you move it back and forth on the ground. Whenever it gets to their feet, they must **jump over it**.

Step 3: The adult should start by moving the jump rope **slowly,** back and forth along the ground. As the child gets better, chant the following chant. Move the jump rope faster when the adult says the word **"faster"**. When the adult says **"stop"** – stop moving the jump rope:

Chant:
I'm jumping, jumping oh so slow.
I'm jumping, jumping oh so fast.
Faster, faster I am almost flying!
Jumping, jumping STOP!

Step 4: Repeat step 3 for as many times as you like!

Activity #1: Glitter "G"

Materials Needed:
- ☐ Any color glitter
- ☐ Elmer's Glue
- ☐ Q-tip
- ☐ Paper Cup (small)
- ☐ Blank Piece of White Paper
- ☐ Black Marker

Instructions:

Step 1: The adult should use a black marker to draw a large "**G**" on a piece of blank paper.

Step 2: The adult should put two tablespoons of Elmer's **g**lue into a small paper cup.

Step 3: Tell your child to dip the Q-tip into the glue and trace the "**G**".

Step 4: The adult should put two tablespoons of **g**litter on the top right corner of the "**G**" paper.

Step 5: Encourage the child to use their fingers to sprinkle the **g**litter all over the lines of glue.

Step 6: Allow the "**G**" to dry overnight.

Activity #2: Clay "G"

Materials Needed:
- Oven
- Clay Materials (see recipe)

Instructions:

Step 1: The adult and child should make Clay (see recipe in Appendix A) together.

Step 2: Once made, roll the clay out in a long rope.

Step 3: Form the clay into the letter "**G**".

Step 4: Bake the clay as described in the recipe.

Activity #3: Clay "G" Decoration

Materials Needed:
- Baked "G" from Activity #2 (see above)
- Watercolors
- Optional: Sequins or glitter and glue

Instructions:

Step 1: Place the clay "**G**" on a baking tray lined with wax paper.

Step 2: Encourage the child to use watercolors and a paintbrush to paint the clay letter. If desired, provide the child with sequins or glitter and glue, allowing them to decorate the letter.

Step 3: Place the project on a shelf overnight to dry.

Activity #4: Go, Go, Stop

Materials Needed:
- Ten (10) Pieces of Blank White Printer Paper cut into ¼ sheets.
- One (1) Green Marker
- One (1) Red Marker
- One (1) Blank Piece of White Paper

Instructions:

Step 1: The adult should use a red marker to write one large "S" on seven of the ¼ sheets of white paper.

Step 2: The adult should use a green marker to write a large "**G**" on each of the remaining of 33 quarter sheets of white paper.

Step 3: Make a trail throughout your home or in an outdoor area, placing the "**G**" squares and the "S" squares randomly throughout the trail.

Step 4: Tell the child that the **g**reen "**G**" means "**g**o" and the red "S" means "stop".

Step 5: Tell the child to follow the trail by jumping to each square. If the square has a red "S", they must stop on that square and count to three before continuing.

Step 6: Ready, set, **G**O! The adult should assist the child throughout the process.

Activity #5: Grouping Like Items

Materials Needed:
- An indoor or outdoor space where the child can look for items by category.

Instructions:

Step 1: Tell the child they're going to go on a search for items that can be **g**rouped into categories which start with the letter "**g**".

Step 2: Tell the child to find five items that are **G**reen.

Step 3: Tell the child to find five items that are **G**ray.

Step 4: Tell the child to find five items that **G**row.

Step 5: Tell the child to find five items that are **G**rand.

Step 6: Tell the child to find five items that **G**o.

Step 7: Tell the child to find five items that are on the **G**round.

Step 8: Can the child think of any more "groups" of items that start with "**G**".

Activity #1: Head Hunt

Materials Needed:
- ☐ One (1) Piece of Paper
- ☐ One (1) Wet Cloth
- ☐ One (1) Pen
- ☐ One (1) Black Marker
- ☐ One (1) Color of Water based, non-toxic paint.
- ☐ One (1) Paper or Plastic plate

Instructions:

Step 1: Use a black marker to draw an "**H**" on a large piece paper.

Step 2: Ask the child to name what is on their **H**ead?

Step 3: Tell the child that their nose is on their **H**ead.

Step 4: Place some drops of water based, non-toxic paint onto a paper plate.

Step 5: Have the child dip the tip of their nose (that is on their **h**ead) into the paint and make nose prints on the "**H**".

Step 6: When the child is done nose printing the "**H**", have them wipe off the tip of their nose with the wet cloth.

Activity #2: Clay "H"

Materials Needed:
- ☐ Oven
- ☐ Clay Materials (see recipe)

Instructions:

Step 1: The Adult and Child should make Clay (see recipe in Appendix A) together.

Step 2: Once made, roll the clay out into a long rope.

Step 3: Form the clay into the letter "**H**".

Step 4: Bake the clay as described in the recipe.

Activity #3: Clay "H" Decoration

Materials Needed:
- ☐ Baked "**H**" from Activity #2 (see above)
- ☐ Watercolors
- ☐ Optional: Sequins or glitter and glue

Instructions:

Step 1: Place the clay "**H**" on a baking tray lined with wax paper.

Step 2: Encourage the child to use watercolors and a paintbrush to paint the clay letter. If desired, provide the child with sequins or glitter and glue, allowing them to decorate the letter.

Step 3: Place the project on a shelf overnight to dry.

Activity #4: Hammer "H"

Materials Needed:
- ☐ One (1) Plastic **H**ammer (child's toy) **or** 16.9 ounce water bottle (full) with lid.
- ☐ One (1) Foam square/rectangle (can be found in the artificial flower department of a craft store)
- ☐ One (1) Package of Golf Ball Tees
- ☐ One (1) Black Marker

Instructions:

Step 1: Using a black marker, have an adult make a large outline of an "**H**" on the foam shape.

Step 2: Allow the child to hammer the golf ball tees in the shape of the "**H**" drawn on the foam shape. If there is no plastic children's **h**ammer available, have the child use a filled 16.9 ounce water bottle to **h**ammer the golf tees in.

Activity #5: Hiding Hints

Materials Needed:
- ☐ Five (5) to Ten (1) dolls, action figures, stuffed animals or familiar objects
- ☐ A large box that the items can hide in.
- ☐ A Black bag that all of the items can fit inside at the same time.

Instructions:

Step 1: This game is full of "Hints" for the objects that are "Hiding". The adult should collect five to ten items from around the home that the child is familiar with. These can include baby dolls, stuffed animals, food items, clothing items, etc. Place all of the collected items in a black plastic bag so the child can't see what is inside.

Step 2: Sit down on the floor and tell the child to close their eyes.

Step 3: Once their eyes are closed put one item underneath the box so the item is hiding.

Step 4: Give the child up to three hints about the object that is hiding under the box and see if the child can guess what it is.

Example:

>   **Item** – Shoes
>
>> **Hint #1** – This item goes on your feet.
>> **Hint #2** – This item sometimes gets dirty by things on the ground.
>> **Hint #3** – This item has a tongue and a heel.

Step 5 – If the child guesses what the item is, have them lift the box off the item and place the item to them. If they didn't guess what it was, pick up the box and put the item next to you.

Step 6 – Repeat steps 4 and 5 until all items have been "guessed".

Step 7 – Encourage the child to count how many objects that are next to them.

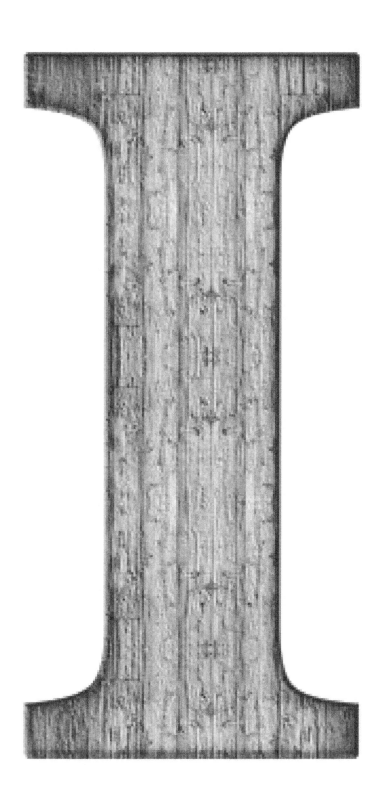

Activity #1: Ice Print "I"

Materials Needed:
- Paper
- Two or Three Ice Cubes
- Finger Paints
- Black Marker

Instructions:

Step 1: Using a black marker, have an adult draw an "I" on a large piece of paper.

Step 2: Encourage the child to dip the ice cubes into the finger paint, then use the painted ice to trace the "I".

 Activity #2: Clay "I"

Materials Needed:
- Oven
- Clay Materials (see recipe)

Instructions:

Step 1: The adult and child should make Clay (see recipe in Appendix A) together.

Step 2: Once made, roll the clay out into a long rope.

Step 3: Form the clay into the letter "I".

Step 4: Bake the clay as described in the recipe.

© JDEducational Curriculum Series: Level 2 Module 1

Activity #3: Clay "I" Decoration

Materials Needed:
- Baked "I" from Activity #2 (see above)
- Watercolors
- Optional: Sequins or glitter and glue

Instructions:

Step 1: Place the clay "I" on a baking tray lined with wax paper.

Step 2: Encourage your child to use watercolors and a paintbrush to paint the clay letter. If desired, provide the child with sequins or glitter and glue, allowing them to decorate the letter.

Step 3: Place the project on a shelf overnight to dry.

Activity #4: Ice Cream "I"

Materials Needed:
- One (1) Brown Piece of Construction Paper
- Crayons or Markers (Any color)
- One (2) White Pieces of Construction Paper
- Three (3) Black Pieces of Construction Paper
- One (1) Package of crayons or markers
- One (1) Glue Stick
- One (1) Pen
- One (1) Pair of Child-sized scissors

Instructions:

Step 1: Today we're going to create our own **ice cream cones**. Yum!

Step 2: The adult should draw **three large triangles** on one piece of **brown construction paper**.

Step 3: The adult should **draw six circles** on the white pieces of construction paper (**three circles on each piece**).

Step 4: Using child-safe scissors, encourage the child to cut out the circles and triangles.

Step 5: Tell the child the **brown triangles** are the **ice cream cones** and the **circles** are going to be **the ice cream.**

Step 6: Encourage the child to **color each white circle a "flavor" of ice cream**. They can create flavors by using any of the markers or crayon colors they have (**Example: Red = Strawberry flavor**).

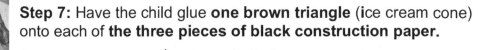

Step 7: Have the child glue **one brown triangle** (ice cream cone) onto each of **the three pieces of black construction paper.**

Step 8: Using the colored circles (ice cream scoops) have the child **build three different ice cream combinations**, by gluing the circles above the triangle.

Ask your child to build a one scoop, a two scoop and a three-scoop ice cream cone, using all of the circles. **One colored circle** equals **one scoop of ice cream**.

Step 9: When the child has finished building each ice cream cone, have the child come up with a **name for each flavor of ice cream** that they created. Write the flavor on the corresponding ice cream circle.

Activity #5: Ice Melting

Note: *This activity requires 24-hour prep time. See step 1.*

Materials Needed:
- One (1) empty ½ gallon milk container
- One (1) freezer
- Two (1) small eye dropper or turkey baster
- Two (2) tablespoons of salt
- One (1) small plastic bin, large enough to fit the empty 1 gallon milk container inside of
- One (1) packet of two or three different food coloring drops
- Three (3) small paper or plastic cups
- One (1) Spoon

Instructions:

Step 1: Fill the empty ½ gallon milk container with water and put it in the freezer.

Step 2: Twenty-four (24) hours later the adult should take the milk container out of the freezer. Using scissors, the adult should cut the carton off of the ice block.

Step 3: Place the large block of ice in a small plastic bin.

Step 4: Place one drop of each food color into each small paper or plastic cup (ex: **one blue drop** in one cup, **one red drop** in another cup and **one green drop** in the third cup).

Step 5: Put one tablespoon of salt into **each cup** with food coloring.

Step 6: Pour ¼ cup of water **into each cup** with salt. Mix all ingredients with a spoon.

Step 7: Tell your child that you are going to melt the large block of ice and make **rainbow water**.

Step 8: Have your child squeeze the eyedropper or turkey baster to fill it up with colored water.

Step 9: Ask them to empty the eyedropper or turkey baster, pushing the colored water onto the large block of ice. Watch how the salt water melts the ice. Continue until the block of ice is melted.

Note: This activity could last for several days. If the child seems tired of this activity, place the ice into the freezer and store the cups of colored salt water on the counter. This activity can be repeated as many times as desired using the same cups of salt water.

Activity #1: "J" Jar

Materials Needed:
- One (1) sale paper
- One (1) pair of child-safe scissors
- One (1) small mason jar or plastic jar (does not need to have a lid)

Instructions:

Step 1: Have the child look through the sale paper and find the letter **J**. Whenever they find the letter "**J**", tell them to use child safe scissors to cut them out.

Step 2: Encourage the child to place all of the "**J**'s" that they find into the "**j**ar".

Activity #2: Clay "J"

Materials Needed:
- Oven
- Clay Materials (see recipe)

Instructions:

Step 1: The Adult and Child should make Clay (see recipe in Appendix A) together.

Step 2: Once made, roll the clay out into a long rope.

Step 3: Form the clay into the letter "**J**".

Step 4: Bake the clay as described in the recipe.

Activity #3: Clay "J" Decoration

Materials Needed:
- Baked "J" from Activity #2 (see above)
- Watercolors
- Optional: Sequins or glitter and glue

Instructions:

Step 1: Place the clay "**J**" on a baking tray lined with wax paper.

Step 2: Encourage your child to use watercolors and a paintbrush to paint the clay letter. If desired, provide the child with sequins or glitter and glue, allowing them to decorate the letter.

Step 3: Place the project on a shelf overnight to dry.

Activity #4: J is for Jelly

Materials Needed:
- Two (2) Tablespoons of Your Favorite Family Jelly
- One (1) Piece of bread or a cracker
- One (1) Plastic Knife
- One (1) Paper Plate

Instructions:

Step 1: Scoop two tablespoons of your favorite **j**elly or **j**am onto a paper plate.

Step 2: Place a plain slice of bread or a large cracker next to the **j**elly.

Step 3: Direct the child to use the plastic knife and **j**elly to write a "**J**" onto the bread or cracker.

Step 4: Eat it when finished.

Activity #5: "J" is for Jumping

Materials Needed:
- One (1) Roll of painters tape
- One (1) Open space available for jumping.

Instructions:

Step 1: The adult should place a **two-foot, straight line of painter's tape** on the carpet or tile.

Step 2: Tell your child that this is a line for **J**umping. **J**umping starts with "**J**".

Step 3: Tell your child that they are to **j**ump over the line while you sing the following song. When you say the word **stop**, the should **freeze** in place!

Step 4: Start singing the following song and allow the child to start **j**umping (to the tune "Are you Sleeping").

- JUMPING, JUMPING,
- JUMPING, JUMPING,
- STOP, STOP, STOP,
- STOP, STOP, STOP,
- JUMPING, JUMPING, JUMPING,
- JUMPING, JUMPING, JUMPING,
- NOW WE STOP! NOW WE STOP!

Step 5: Repeat step 4 for as long as you like!

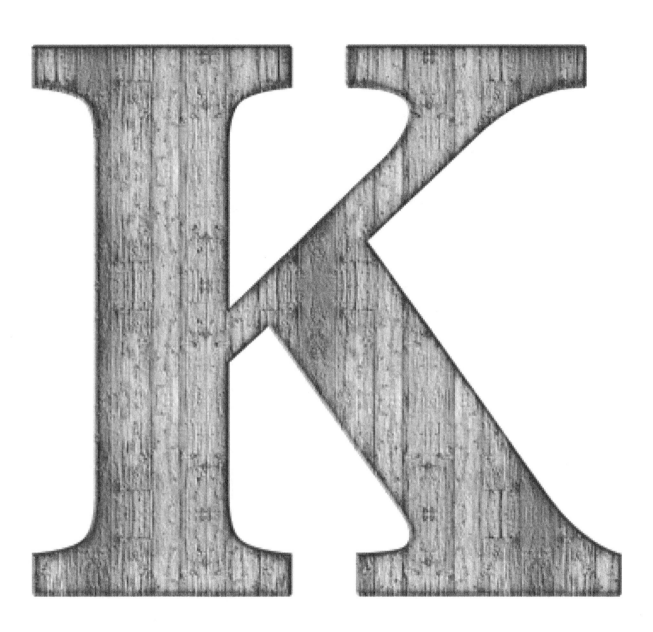

✎ Activity #1: Key Painting "K"

Materials Needed:
- Paper
- One Key
- Finger Paints
- Black Marker

Instructions:

Step 1: Using a black marker, have an adult draw a "**K**" on a large piece of paper.

Step 2: Encourage the child to dip end of a **k**ey into finger paint, then use the key to trace the "**K**".

✎ Activity #2: Clay "K"

Materials Needed:
- Oven
- Clay Materials (see recipe)

Instructions:

Step 1: The adult and child should make Clay (see recipe in Appendix A) together.

Step 2: Once made, roll the clay out into a long line.

Step 3: Form the clay into the letter "**K**".

Step 4: Bake the clay as described in the recipe.

✎ Activity #3: Clay "K" Decoration

Materials Needed:
- Baked "K" from Activity #2 (see above)
- Watercolors
- Optional: Sequins or glitter and glue

Instructions:

Step 1: Place the clay "**K**" on a baking tray lined with wax paper.

Step 2: Encourage the child to use watercolors and a paintbrush to paint the clay letter. If desired, provide the child with sequins or glitter and glue, allowing them to decorate the letter.

Step 3: Place the project on a shelf overnight to dry.

© JDEducational Curriculum Series: Level 2 Module 1

Activity #4: Kitchen "K"

Materials Needed:
- One (1) Piece of Paper
- One (1) Yellow Highlighter
- One (1) Package of crayons or markers
- One (1) Pen or Pencil

Instructions:

Step 1: Today we're going to look around the **K**itchen and find everything that begins with the letter "**K**".

Step 2: The adult should use a yellow highlighter to write the word "**K**itchen" at the top of a piece of paper.

Step 3: The adult should walk around the **k**itchen with the child. Using a yellow highlighter, the adult should write down everything their child finds that starts with the letter "**K**".

The most common items are: **K**etchup, **K**ool-aide, **K**ettle, **K**abob, **K**ale, **K**ellogg's (cereal brand), **K**ey Lime Pie, **K**idney Beans, **K**ing crab, Hershey's **K**isses, **K**it **K**at bar, **K**iwi, **K**ix cereal, **K**londike bars, **K**raft cheese, Sour **K**raut, **K**rispy **K**reme Donuts or **K**ung Pao Chicken).

Step 4: Once completed, ask your child to use a pencil to trace all of the words written in yellow highlighter.

Step 5: Ask your child to count how many items they found.

Activity #5: Kick Ball

Materials Needed:
- One (1) 12 inch ball or larger
- One (1) outdoor or indoor space where kicking a ball would be safe

Instructions:

Step 1: The child and an adult should face each other and stand 5 to 6 feet apart.

Step 2: The adult should **ki**ck the ball to the child and say a word that starts with "**k**" (Example: **K**itten, **K**ite, **K**ind, etc)

Step 3: The child should **ki**ck the ball back to the adult and say a word that starts with "**k**".

Step 4: Ask the child to count how many times they **k**ick the ball back and forth.

Optional: Use a timer to time how many back and forth "**k**-word **k**icks" you can complete in a minute?

Activity #1: Lip "L"

Materials Needed:
- Paper
- One stick of 'Lipstick'
- Black Marker

Instructions:

Step 1: Have an adult write a large letter "**L**" on a blank piece of white paper.

Step 2: Next, help the child put lipstick (any color) on their lips.

Step 3: Encourage the child to kiss the lines on the "**L**" that is written on the paper. Can they see their "lip" prints?

Activity #2: Clay "L"

Materials Needed:
- Oven
- Clay Materials (see recipe)

Instructions:

Step 1: The adult and child should make Clay (see recipe in Appendix A) together.

Step 2: Once made, roll the clay out into a long rope.

Step 3: Form the clay into the letter "**L**".

Step 4: Bake the clay as described in the recipe.

Activity #3: Clay "L" Decoration

Materials Needed:
- Baked "L" from Activity #2 (see above)
- Watercolors
- Optional: Sequins or glitter and glue

Instructions:

Step 1: Place the clay "**L**" on a baking tray lined with wax paper.

Step 2: Encourage your child to use watercolors and a paintbrush to paint the clay letter. If desired, provide the child with sequins or glitter and glue, allowing them to decorate the letter.

Step 3: Place the project on a shelf overnight to dry.

Activity #4: L is for Lemonade

Materials Needed:
- Two (2) Lemons
- One (1) Tablespoon of Sugar
- One (1) Plastic cup
- One (1) Spoon for mixing
- One (1) Knife

Instructions:

Step 1: Have an adult use a knife to cut two lemons in half. Place the knife out of reach of the child.

Step 2: Encourage your child to squeeze the lemon juice over the plastic cup.

Step 3: Ask your child what they think the lemon juice will taste like?

Step 4: Once the juice from both lemons is squeezed out, have your child taste the lemon juice. Ask them to describe the taste (bitter and sour).

Step 5: Direct the child to put two tablespoons of sugar into the cup and mix it together with the spoon.

Step 6: Now allow the child to drink the lemonade! Ask the child how the lemon juice tastes with sugar. **Lemons are sour and sugar is sweet**.

Activity #5: "L" is for Leap Frog

Materials Needed:
- One (1) Roll of painter's tape
- One (1) Open space available for jumping.

Instructions:

Step 1: The adult should place four, six-inch lines of painters tape, on the floor. Each line should be one foot apart from each other.

| 6" | 6" | 6" |

Step 2: Tell the child that these lines are for "Leaping" over.

Step 3: Have your child bend their knees, and touch the floor, lowering into a squatting position.

Step 4: Tell them to push off the floor with their hands and feet at the same time, jumping over the tape and landing on the other side of the line. They should land in the same squatting position.

Continue leaping over the line for as they would like!

Activity #1: "M"

Materials Needed:
- ☐ Paper
- ☐ Black Marker, Crayon or Pen
- ☐ Glue
- ☐ One piece of Blue Construction Paper
- ☐ One piece of Red Construction Paper
- ☐ One piece of Green Construction Paper
- ☐ Child safe scissors

Instructions:

Step 1: Have an adult draw a large "**M**" on a large piece of paper.

Step 2: Have the child use child-safe scissors to cut tiny pieces of blue, red and green pieces of paper.

Step 3: Tell the child to "**M**ix" the pieces of paper together.

Step 4: Allow the child to help you put dots of glue on top of the letter "**M**".

Step 5: Tell the child place the pieces of paper "**M**ix" onto the glue.

Activity #2: Clay "M"

Materials Needed:
- ☐ Oven
- ☐ Clay Materials (see recipe)

Instructions:

Step 1: The adult and child should make Clay (see recipe at appendix A) together.

Step 2: Once made, roll the clay out into a long rope.

Step 3: Form the clay into the letter "**M**".

Step 4: Bake the clay as described in the recipe.

Activity #3: Clay "M" Decoration

Materials Needed:
- ☐ Baked "M" from Activity #2 (see above)
- ☐ Watercolors
- ☐ Optional: Sequins or glitter and glue

Instructions:

Step 1: Place the clay "**M**" on a baking tray lined with wax paper.

Step 2: Encourage the child to use watercolors and a paintbrush to paint the clay letter. If desired, provide the child with sequins or glitter and glue, allowing them to decorate the letter.

Step 3: Place the project on a shelf overnight to dry.

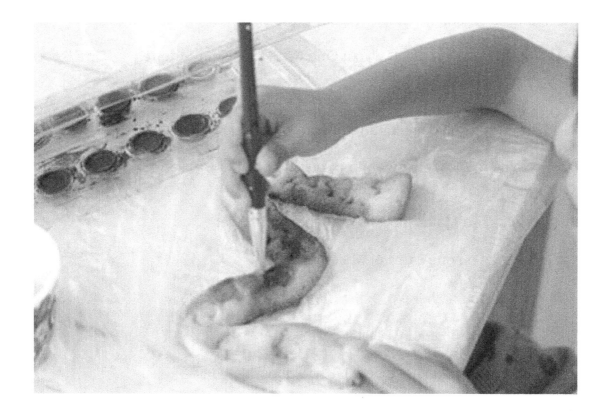

Activity #4: Machine Match

Materials Needed:
- ☐ One (1) Piece of Red Paper
- ☐ One (1) Piece of Blue Paper
- ☐ One (1) Piece of Green Paper
- ☐ One (1) Piece of Orange Paper
- ☐ One (1) Glue Stick
- ☐ One (1) Adult sized scissors
- ☐ Four (4) Pieces of white paper.
- ☐ One (1) Black Marker
- ☐ One (1) Yellow Highlighter

Instructions:

Step 1: Using scissors, the adult will cut **One Circle** ⃝, **One Square** ☐, **One Rectangle** ▭ and **One Triangle** ▲ out of the **Red Piece of Paper**.

Step 2: Using scissors, the adult will cut **One Circle** ⃝, **One Square** ☐, **One Rectangle** ▭ and **One Triangle** ▲ out the **Blue Piece of Paper.**

Step 3: Using scissors, the adult will cut **One Circle** ⃝, **One Square** ☐, **One Rectangle** ▭ and **One Triangle** ▲ out of the **Green Piece of Paper**.

Step 4: Using scissors, the adult will cut **One Circle** ⃝, **One Square** ☐, **One Rectangle** ▭ and **One Triangle** ▲ out of the **Orange Piece of Paper**.

Step 5: Place the four sheets **of white paper** in front of the child.

Step 6: Have the child **M**atch the colored paper by **shape**:

- All 4 squares on one piece of white paper ☐
- All 4 circles on another piece of white paper ⃝
- All 4 rectangles on another piece of white paper ▭
- All 4 triangles on another piece of white paper. ▲

Step 7: Next, have the child **M**atch all of the shapes by **color**:

- All 4 **green shapes** together
- All 4 **red shapes** together
- All 4 **blue shapes** together
- All 4 **orange shapes** together.

Step 8: Allow the child to build **4 different M**achines with the **M**atched colors:

>**Example:** Glue the **red shapes** to one piece of paper, in any order that they want, to make a Mighty Machine.

Step 9: Repeat step 10 with the rest of the colored shapes (All **green shapes** together, all **blue shapes** together and all **orange shapes** together).

Step 10: The adult should use a **yellow highlighter** to write the letter "**M**" on the square of each "Machine" paper.

Step 11: Tell the child to trace the letter "**M**" with a black marker.

Activity #5: Music March

Materials Needed:
- ☐ A large space, inside or outside, big enough for movement activities.
- ☐ One (1) Yellow piece of paper
- ☐ One (1) Blue piece of paper
- ☐ One (1) Roll of scotch tape.

Instructions:

Step 1: Tell the child that they are going to **m**ake **m**usic with their feet.

Step 2: Tell the child to tear off a piece of **yellow paper**.

Step 3: The adult should give the child two pieces of tape and help them tape the **yellow** piece of paper to their **right shoe.**

Step 4: Tell the child to tear off a piece of **blue paper.**

Step 5: The adult should give the child two pieces of tape and help them tape the **blue piece of paper** to their **left shoe**.

Step 6: Tell the child to listen so they can hear the beat. When the adult says **"blue"**, the child should stomp their **left foot**. When the adult says **"yellow"** the child should stop their **right foot.**

Step 7: Now it is time to do the color **M**arch!

Step 8: The adult should say the following patterns. The child can **m**ove while **m**arching!

- Yellow (right foot stomp); **Y**ellow **(**right foot stomp); **Blue** (left foot stomp); **Blue** (left foot stomp); **Y**ellow (right foot stomp); **Blue** (left foot stomp); **Blue** (left foot stomp). **Repeat pattern three times.**

- Yellow (right foot stomp); **Blue** (left foot stomp); **Yellow** (right foot stomp); **Yellow** (right foot stomp); **Blue** (left foot stomp); **Yellow** (right foot stomp); **Yellow** (right foot stomp). **Repeat pattern three times.**

Step 9: What other patterns can you make up? Have the child say the patterns they want to **m**arch.

> **Take it to the Next Level:**
>
> Change colors of the paper on the child's feet and try more patterns **OR** place two more colors in the pattern (tape one color on each of their hands). Now they can follow four color **m**arch (stomp, stomp with their feet) and tap, tap (with their hand colors).

Activity #1: Number Nine

Materials Needed:
- ☐ One (1) Piece of Paper
- ☐ Nine (9) Pom-Pom Craft Balls
- ☐ One (1) Black Marker
- ☐ One (1) Bottle of Elmer's Glue

Instructions:

Step 1: The adult shall draw an "**N**" on a large piece of blank paper using the black marker.

Step 2: The adult should ask the child to help them count from One to **N**ine.

Step 3: The adult should place **n**ine drops of Elmer's' glue on the letter "**N**", with one inch between each drop.

Step 4: Ask the child to place one Pom-Pom on each of the glue drops.

Step 5: Have the child count the Pomp-Poms (**N**ine).

Step 6: Remind the child that the **N**umber **N**ine starts with the letter "**N**".

Activity #2: Clay "N"

Materials Needed:
- ☐ Oven
- ☐ Clay Materials (see recipe)

Instructions:

Step 1: The adult and child should make Clay (see recipe in Appendix A) together.

Step 2: Once made, roll the clay out into a long rope.

Step 3: Form the clay into the letter **"N"**.

Step 4: Bake the clay as described in the recipe.

Activity #3: Clay "N" Decoration

Materials Needed:
- ☐ Baked "**N**" from Activity #2 (see above)
- ☐ Watercolors
- ☐ Optional: Sequins or glitter and glue

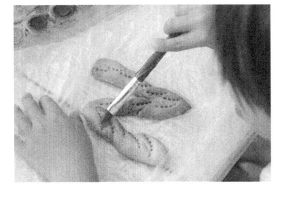

Instructions:

Step 1: Place the clay "**N**" on a baking tray lined with wax paper.

Step 2: Encourage the child to use watercolors and a paintbrush to paint the clay letter.
If desired, provide the child with sequins or glitter and glue, allowing them to decorate the letter.

Step 3: Place the project on a shelf overnight to dry.

Activity #4: "Next to" Storybook

Materials Needed:
- ☐ One (1) box of Crayons
- ☐ One (1) Pen
- ☐ Ten (10) Piece of Blank Paper

Instructions:

Step 1: Sit down with the child and tell them that together you're going create a story called "**N**ext To…"

Step 2: The adult will write the word "**N**ext to.." on the bottom of each piece of paper.

Step 3: Tell the child they're going to tell the adult an object that is **n**ext to them.

Step 4: The adult should start the story by saying "I see (child's name). (Object or person) is **n**ext to them".

© JDEducational Curriculum Series: Level 2 Module 1

Step 5: On the top of the first piece of paper, the adult should write the name of the child or the object (or person) that is "**n**ext to" the child.

Example: Dog

Step 6: Next, ask the child to look around and say what is "**n**ext to" the person/object that was said in step 4.

Step 7: The adult should write the name of the object or person the child said on the "**n**ext" piece of paper.

Example: Dog is next to Trashcan

Step 8: Next, ask the child to look around and say what is "**n**ext to" the person/object that was said in step 5.

Step 9: The adult should write the name of the object or person the child said on the "**n**ext" piece of paper.

Example: Trashcan is next to Table.

Step 10: Continue step 8 and 9, until the child has stated what is **n**ext to the previous item 10 times (until all of the pieces of white paper has an object written on the top).

Step 11: Ask the child to draw a picture of each item they named on the paper with the corresponding words.

Step 12: The adult should put the pages in order to make a book. Start with page that has the child and the first item drawn on it.

Example:
Page 1: Child
Page 2: Dog
Page 3: Dog is next to Trashcan
Page 4: Trashcan is next to Table
Etc.

Step 13: The adult should then place the rest of the pieces of paper, in order from when they were created, behind the piece of paper in step 10.

Step 14: The adult should then attach the pages together with a staple.

Step 15: Allow the child to read the story they created!

© JDEducational Curriculum Series: Level 2 Module 1

✎ Activity #5: Oh so "Nice"

Materials Needed:
- ☐ One (1) piece of paper
- ☐ One (1) pen

Instructions:

Step 1: Sit with the child and tell them that together you're going to come up with a list of "**N**ice" things they can do for their family and friends.

Step 2: The adult should write down the names of everyone in the child's immediate family (including grandma's and grandpa's, aunt's and uncle's, sister's and brother's, cousins' and parents).

Step 3: Now tell the child to come up with something "**N**ice" to do this month for each of the family members listed.

Step 4: Help the child come up something **n**ice for each family member. Write what the "**n**ice" thing is **n**ext to each family members **n**ame.

Examples could include:

- o Grandma- Give a hug
- o Sister - Write a card
- o Aunt - Bake cookies
- o Neighbor - Visit
- o Friend - Call
- o Daddy - Draw a picture for

Step 5: Over the **n**ext month, help the child complete all of the "**n**ice" things on the list.

© JDEducational Curriculum Series: Level 2 Module 1

Activity #1: Object "O"

Materials Needed:
- ☐ A small "**O**bject" that is in the shape of an "**O**" (Cotton ball, Penny, etc.)
- ☐ One (1) Piece of paper
- ☐ One (1) Black Marker
- ☐ One (1) **O**range Crayon or colored pencil

Instructions:

Step 1: Have an adult draw an "**O**" on a large piece of paper.

Step 2: Encourage the child to trace the **O**bject with the **O**range crayon (or colored pencil).

Activity #2: Clay "O"

Materials Needed:
- ☐ Oven
- ☐ Clay Materials (see recipe)

Instructions:

Step 1: The adult and child should make Clay (see recipe in Appendix A) together.

Step 2: Once made, roll the clay out into a long rope.

Step 3: Form the clay into the letter "**O**".

Step 4: Bake the clay as described in the recipe.

Activity #3: Clay "O" Decoration

Materials Needed:
- ☐ Baked "O" from Activity #2 (see above)
- ☐ Watercolors
- ☐ Optional: Sequins or glitter and glue

Instructions:

Step 1: Place the clay "**O**" on a baking tray lined with wax paper.

Step 2: Encourage the child to use watercolors and a paintbrush to paint the clay letter. If desired, provide the child with sequins or glitter and glue, allowing them to decorate the letter.

Step 3: Place the project on a shelf overnight to dry.

© JDEducational Curriculum Series: Level 2 Module 1

Activity #4: Open the Shoebox

Materials Needed:
- ☐ One (1) Empty Shoebox
- ☐ Twenty-Six (26) 3x5 cards (Any Color)
- ☐ One (1) Green piece of paper
- ☐ One (1) Black Marker

Instructions:

Step 1: The adult should use the black marker to write all of the letters of the alphabet (from A to Z) on the 3x5 cards. **Write one letter on each card.**

Step 2: Have the child sit on the floor (or at a table) **in front of the shoebox**.

Step 3: The adult should sit on the floor (or at a table) **behind the shoebox.**

Step 4: Using the black marker, the adult should write the word "**O**pen" on the green piece of paper.

Step 5: The adult should place one index card (with any letter on it) inside the shoebox. Make sure the lid is placed back on the shoebox.

Step 6: Allow the child to hold the green piece of paper from step 4.

Step 7: The adult should tell the child four words that start with the letter the adult is hiding in the shoebox.

> **Example** (Letter T) – truck, train, two, time.

Step 8: Ask the child if they can guess what letter is in the shoebox, based on the words the adult said. Have them sound out the words slowly to hear that first sound.

Step 9: When the child is ready to find out if they were right, have them hold up the "**O**pen" sign from Step 4 and say the word "**O**pen!".

Step 10: The adult should open the lid to the box so the child can see if they guessed the correct letter.

Step 11: Repeat Step 5 through Step 10 for all of the letters of the alphabet.

Step 12: Repeat the entire activity as often as the child would like.

Activity #5: Over the Objects

Materials Needed:
- [ ] One (1) Pillow
- [ ] One (1) Piece of Paper
- [ ] One (1) Book
- [ ] One (1) Paper Bag (or Canvas Grocery Bag)

Instructions:

Step 1: The adult should place the **o**bjects from the material list on the floor, two feet apart from each other.

Step 2: Tell the child they're going to jump "**O**ver" Each "**O**bject" on the floor, while saying the word "**O**ver".

Step 3: Once the child has jumped **o**ver all of the **o**bjects, have them hop on **O**ne foot three times.

Step 4: Have the child turn around and repeat Step 3.

Step 5: Repeat Step 3 and Step 4 as much as they would like.

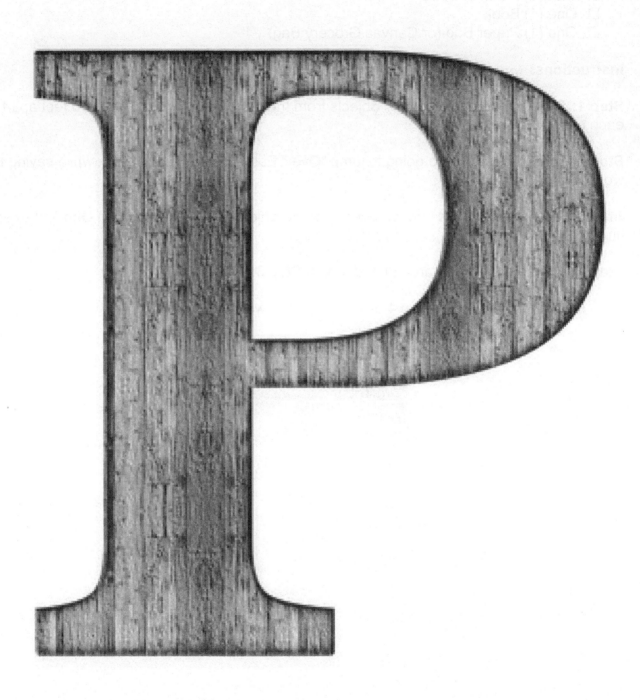

Activity #1: Pieces of P

Materials Needed:
- ☐ Two (2) Piece of Paper
- ☐ One (1) glue stick
- ☐ One (1) Black Marker
- ☐ One (1) Purple Marker

Instructions:

Step 1: Draw a "**P**" on a large piece of blank paper with a black marker

Step 2: Draw a "**P**" on a large piece of paper with a **P**urple marker.

Step 3: Allow the child to tear the **P**urple **P** into small **P**ieces with their fingers.

Step 4: Ask the child to use a glue stick to glue the **P**urple **P** Pieces onto the **P** that was made with a black marker.

Activity #2: Clay "P"

Materials Needed:
- ☐ Oven
- ☐ Clay Materials (see recipe)

Instructions:

Step 1: The adult and child should make Clay (see recipe in Appendix A) together.

Step 2: Once made, roll the clay out into a long rope.

Step 3: Form the clay into the letter "**P**".

Step 4: Bake the clay as described in the recipe.

Activity #3: Clay "P" Decoration

Materials Needed:
- ☐ Baked "P" from Activity #2 (see above)
- ☐ Watercolors
- ☐ Optional: Sequins or glitter and glue

Instructions:

Step 1: Place the clay "**P**" on a baking tray lined with wax paper.

Step 2: Encourage the child to use watercolors and a paintbrush to paint the clay letter. If desired, provide the child with sequins or glitter and glue, allowing them to decorate the letter.

Step 3: Place the **p**roject on a shelf overnight to dry.

Activity #4: A Picnic with my Puppy

Materials Needed:
- ☐ Grocery Store Ads
- ☐ Pet Store Ads
- ☐ Child Sized Scissors
- ☐ Five (5) paper plates
- ☐ Five (5) paper or plastic cups
- ☐ One (1) glue stick
- ☐ One (1) printed out picture of a puppy or stuffed animal puppy
- ☐ One (1) printed out picture of a parrot or stuffed animal parrot
- ☐ One (1) printed out picture of a penguin or stuffed animal penguin
- ☐ One (1) printed out picture of a porcupine or stuffed animal porcupine

Instructions:

Step 1: Tell the child they're going to **P**lan a **P**icnic for them and a **P**uppy.

Step 2: Allow the child to use the child size/child safe scissors to cut out **p**ictures out of the **p**et store ads. The pictures should be of items they would like to take on their **p**icnic. Make sure they cut out some **p**ictures of food and drinks to share with the **p**uppy.

Step 3: Once the child is done cutting out the objects, have them place the food items they want to eat on one **p**late. Tell them to place some food items on another **p**late for the **p**uppy to eat.

Step 4: **P**lace the **p**icture or stuffed animal **p**uppy in front of the child and have them **p**retend to have a **p**icnic. The **p**uppy can eat off the **p**uppy's **p**late.

Step 5: Oh Look!!! Three more friends want to join the **P**icnic!

Step 6: Place three more **p**aper **p**lates and three more **p**aper or **p**lastic cups near the child.

Step 7: Tell them three more animal friends want to join the **P**retend **P**icnic **P**arty. All of these animal names start with **P**.

Step 8: Give the child the **p**ictures or stuffed animals of the **P**enguin, **P**arrot and **P**orcupine. Tell them to set up the **p**icnic area.

Step 9: Encourage the child to share the food (ad pictures) and drink (ad pictures) with the new friends, by placing some of the pictures in their cups and **p**lates.

Step 10: Does the child have enough food and drink to share with four animal friends? If not, encourage them to cut out more **p**ictures from the pet store and grocery store ad **p**aper.

© JDEducational Curriculum Series: Level 2 Module 1

Step 11: Once the child is done dividing up the food and drinks, have them use the glue stick to glue the food and drinks to each animal's plate and cups. Bon-a-apatite!

✏ Activity #5: Number Pop

Materials Needed:
  ☐ An open space for dancing or jumping

Instructions:

Step 1: Tell the child they're going to turn into **P**opcorn.

Step 2: Tell the child you're going to start counting. Ask them to say a number between one and ten. (If they don't know their numbers, the adult can suggest a number).

Step 3: Tell the child to sit on their knees. Tell them to **p**ut their head on the floor and place their hands in front of them (they should look like they are curled up in a ball). Tell them he/she is now a **P**opcorn Kernel.

Step 4: Tell the child to remember the number they picked in Step 2. When they hear that number, they should jump up, waving their hands above their heads (turn into popcorn) and say "**P**op!".

Step 5: The adult should start counting (in order) from one to the number the child picked in Step 2. If the child doesn't jump up when the adult says the number, then remind them you said the number.

Step 6: Repeat step 2 through 5 picking different numbers each time.

Activity #1: Q-tip "Q"

Materials Needed:
- Paper
- Black Marker, Crayon or Pen
- Glue
- One (1) Q-tip
- One (1) set of Water Color Paints

Instructions:

Step 1: Have an adult draw a large "**Q**" on a large piece of paper.

Step 2: Have the child dip one end of the "**Q**-tip" in the watercolor paint and trace the "**Q**" from Step 1.

Step 3: Allow the child to decorate the letter "**Q**" from step 1 by drawing pictures with the **Q**-tip, once dipped in watercolor.

Activity #2: Clay "Q"

Materials Needed:
- Oven
- Clay Materials (see recipe)

Instructions:

Step 1: The adult and child should make Clay (see recipe at appendix A) together.

Step 2: Once made, roll the clay out into a long rope.

Step 3: Form the clay into the letter "**Q**".

Step 4: Bake the clay as described in the recipe.

✏️ Activity #3: Clay "Q" Decoration

Materials Needed:
- Baked "**Q**" from Activity #2 (see above)
- Watercolors
- Optional: Sequins or glitter and glue

Instructions:

Step 1: Place the clay "**Q**" on a baking tray lined with wax paper.

Step 2: Encourage the child to use watercolors and a paintbrush to paint the clay letter. If desired, provide the child with sequins or glitter and glue, allowing them to decorate the letter.

Step 3: Place the project on a shelf overnight to dry.

✏️ Activity #4: Quail bird sees

Materials Needed:
- One (1) Printed picture of a Quail bird
- Two (2) Pieces of Paper
- One (1) Glue Stick
- One (1) child sized/child safe scissors
- One (1) Black Marker
- One (1) Yellow Highlighter

Instructions:

Step 1: Ask your child to use child-safe scissors to cut out a photo of a **q**uail.

Step 2: Tell your child to glue the picture of the **q**uail onto one piece of paper.

Step 3: The adult should use a black marker to write the words "**Q**uail Bird Sees" above the **Q**uail Bird.

Step 4: The adult should use the black marker to write the words "By (child's name)" below the **Q**uail Bird.

© JDEducational Curriculum Series: Level 2 Module 1

Step 5: Next, have the child trace the words written in Step 3 and Step 4 with a yellow highlighter.

Step 6: Tell the child to close their eyes and pretend they're a **q**uail bird.

Step 7: Ask the child to tell the parent what they see from the sky while they're flying around.

Step 8: The adult should use the black pen or marker to write down what their child says they see on a piece of blank paper.

Step 9: Ask you're the child trace the words that were written in Step 8 with **a yellow highlighter.** Reread the story throughout the week.

✏ Activity #5: The Quiet Walk

Materials Needed:
- A large space, inside or outside, big enough for movement activities.

Instructions:

Step 1: Tell the child they're going to play the **q**uiet game.

Step 2: Ask the child to close their eyes. Tell the child to keep their eyes closed and only open them if they hear you move. Ready, Set… Go!

Step 3: The adult should tiptoe, very **q**uietly, around the room or yard.

Step 4: When the child hears the adult move, they should open their eyes. The adult should say "Not **Q**uiet!" and freeze.

Step 5: Switch roles. The adult should close their eyes and child can move around the designated area being as quiet as a mouse until the adult hears them.

> **Tell the child the following rule:** Whoever is walking around needs to stay within the room or outdoor space they're in (make sure the space is gated, fenced or you're indoors with the doors locked so the child cannot sneak out of the house).

Activity #1: Rainbow Décor

Materials Needed:
- One (1) Box of Crayons
- One (1) Black Marker
- One (1) Piece of Blank Paper

Instructions:

Step 1: The adult should use a black marker to draw a large "**R**" on a piece of blank paper.

Step 2: The adult should use a pencil to write the following color words on the same paper as the letter "**R**":

- **Red**
- **Orange**
- **Yellow**
- **Green**
- **Blue**
- **Purple**

Step 3: Ask the child to trace each color word with the corresponding crayon color (trace the word "red" with a red crayon, etc).

- **Red**
- **Orange**
- **Yellow**
- **Green**
- **Blue**
- **Purple**

Step 4: These are the colors of a **R**ainbow!

Activity #2: Clay "R"

Materials Needed:
- Oven
- Clay Materials (see recipe)

Instructions:

Step 1: The adult and child should make Clay (see recipe in Appendix A) together.

Step 2: Once made, roll the clay out into a long rope.

Step 3: Form the clay into the letter **"R"**.

Step 4: Bake the clay as described in the recipe.

Activity #3: Clay "R" Decoration

Materials Needed:
- Baked "**R**" from Activity #2 (see above)
- Watercolors
- Optional: Sequins or glitter and glue

Instructions:

Step 1: Place the clay "**R**" on a baking tray lined with wax paper.

Step 2: Encourage the child to use watercolors and a paintbrush to paint the clay letter. If desired, provide the child with sequins or glitter and glue, allowing them to decorate the letter.

Step 3: Place the project on a shelf overnight to dry.

Activity #4: The first time I rode in a Car

Materials Needed:
- One (1) box of Crayons
- One (1) Pen
- Ten (2) Piece of Blank Paper

Instructions:

Step 1: Sit with the child and tell them its time to create a story about the **first** time they **r**ode in a car.

Step 2: The adult will write the word "**Ride**" on the top of one piece of paper. Then write down the child's answers to the following questions:

- Ask the child what the color of their car is.
- Ask the child what's in their car.
- Ask the child where they went.
- Ask the child what they saw from the car.
- Ask the child what they were listening to while they were riding in the car.
- Ask the child who was in the car with them.
- Ask the child where they were sitting.
- Ask the child if there is anything else that they remember from their first car ride.

Step 3: Ask the child to use crayons to draw a picture of their first ride in the car.

Activity #5: Round, Round, Rest

Materials Needed:
- One (1) role of painters tape
- Kids Music

Instructions:

Step 1: Tell the child you're going to play the game "**R**ound, **R**ound, **R**est".

Step 2: Using painters tape, the adult should make a large circle on the floor, big enough for the child to lay down in.

Step 3: When the adult plays the kid's music, the child should **R**un around the taped circle.

Step 4: Thirty seconds after the music starts, the adult should pause the music. When the music pauses, have the child lay down in the middle of the circle and **R**est.

Step 5: Repeat Step 3 and Step 4 as many times as you would like.

Activity #1: Sandy "S"

Materials Needed:
- One (1) cup of sand
- One (1) Piece of paper
- One (1) Black Marker
- One (1) Bottle of Elmer's Glue
- One (1) art paint brush
- One (1) plastic/paper bowl

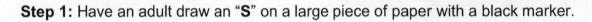

Instructions:

Step 1: Have an adult draw an "**S**" on a large piece of paper with a black marker.

Step 2: The adult should put two tablespoons of Elmer's glue into a plastic/paper bowl.

Step 3: Encourage the child to dip the paintbrush into the glue and trace the "**S**".

Step 4: Let the child use their fingers to sprinkle the **S**and onto the glue.

Step 5: Place the "**S**" up to dry.

Activity #2: Clay "S"

Materials Needed:
- Oven
- Clay Materials (see recipe)

Instructions:

Step 1: The adult and child should make Clay (see recipe in Appendix A) together.

Step 2: Once made, roll the clay out into a long rope.

Step 3: Form the clay into the letter "**S**".

Step 4: Bake the clay as described in the recipe.

Activity #3: Clay "S" Decoration

Materials Needed:
- Baked "**S**" from Activity #2 (see above)
- Watercolors
- Optional: Sequins or glitter and glue

Instructions:

Step 1: Place the clay "**S**" on a baking tray lined with wax paper.

Step 2: Encourage the child to use watercolors and a paintbrush to paint the clay letter. If desired, provide the child with sequins or glitter and glue, allowing them to decorate the letter.

Step 3: Place the project on a shelf overnight to dry.

Activity #4: Stand or Sit

Materials Needed:
- One (1) chair
- One (1) space to stand up

Instructions:

Step 1: Tell the child they're going to **s**tand in the middle of the room, next to the chair.

Step 2: Tell the child that the adult is going to describe some things that people do while **s**tanding up and **s**itting down. When the adult says the following phrases, have the child **s**ay if they would **s**it or **s**tand to complete that task. If they **s**ay **s**it, they should **s**it in the chair. If they **s**ay **s**tand, they should **s**tand next to the chair.

- Riding in a car (**c**hild **s**hould **s**ay "**s**it" and **s**it down)
- Walking through the **s**tore (child **s**hould **s**ay "Stand" and **s**tand up)
- Eating dinner (child **s**hould **s**ay "Sit" and **s**it down)
- Taking a **s**hower (child **s**hould **s**ay "stand" and **s**tand up)

Step 3: What other "**s**tand" and "**s**it" activities can you or the child think of? Repeat step 3 with the activities that you and the child came up with.

Activity #5: Sing, Sing, Sneaky Snake

Materials Needed:
- Five (5) Pieces of Paper
- One (1) Black Marker

Instructions:

Step 1: The adult should use a black marker to write the follow **S**ong Names, writing one **S**ong Name on each piece of paper.

- Twinkle, Twinkle Little Star
- Old MacDonald Had a Farm
- Itsy Bitsy Spider
- B-I-N-G-O
- Row, Row, Row Your Boat

Step 2: Place the five **s**heets of paper on the floor, about 3 to 4 feet between each piece of paper. The papers should **not** be place in a straight line.

Step 3: Tell the child to lie on their **s**tomach, on the floor, and **s**quiggle across the floor like a **s**nake until they touch one of the pieces of paper.

Step 4: Once they reach the paper, ask them to read the name of the **s**ong that is written on that piece of paper.

Step 5: Sing the **s**ong that is on that paper (see next page for words to songs).

Step 6: Repeat Step 3 and Step 4 until all **s**ongs are **s**ung

© JDEducational Curriculum Series: Level 2 Module 1

Songs for Activity S-5

Itsy Bitsy Spider
The itsy bitsy (or eensy weensy) spider
Climbed up the waterspout
Down came the rain
And washed the spider out
Out came the sun
And dried up all the rain
And the itsy bitsy spider
Climbed up the spout again

Row Row Row Your Boat
Row, row, row your boat
Gently down the stream,
Merrily, merrily, merrily, merrily
Life is but a dream

Old MacDonald Had a Farm
Old MACDONALD had a farm
E-I-E-I-O
And on his farm he had a cow
E-I-E-I-O
With a moo moo here
And a moo moo there
Here a moo, there a moo
Everywhere a moo moo
Old MacDonald had a farm
E-I-E-I-O

© JDEducational Curriculum Series: Level 2 Module 1

Twinkle Twinkle Little Star
Twinkle, twinkle, little star,
How I wonder what you are!
Up above the world so high,
Like a diamond in the sky.

B-I-N-G-O
There was a farmer who had a dog,
And Bingo was his name-o.
B-I-N-G-O
B-I-N-G-O
B-I-N-G-O
And Bingo was his name-o.

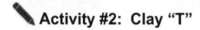 **Activity #1: Toothbrush "T"**

Materials Needed:
- One (1) Piece of Paper
- One (1) old toothbrush
- Two (2) tablespoons of water based, non toxic paint (any color)
- One (1) paper plate

Instructions:

Step 1: Draw a "T" on a large piece of blank paper with a black marker.

Step 2: The adult should put **t**wo **t**ablespoons of water based, not toxic paint, onto a paper plate.

Step 3: Allow the child to paint the "**T**" from step one using a **t**oothbrush.

 **Activity #2: Clay "T"**

Materials Needed:
- Oven
- Clay Materials (see recipe)

Instructions:

Step 1: The adult and child should make Clay (see recipe in Appendix A) together.

Step 2: Once made, roll the clay out into a long line.

Step 3: Form the clay into the letter "**T**".

Step 4: Bake the clay as described in the recipe.

Activity #3: Clay "T" Decoration

Materials Needed:
- Baked "**T**" from Activity #2 (see above)
- Watercolors
- Optional: Sequins or glitter and glue

Instructions:

Step 1: Place the clay "**T**" on a baking tray lined with wax paper.

Step 2: Encourage the child to use watercolors and a paintbrush to paint the clay letter. If desired, provide the child with sequins or glitter and glue, allowing them to decorate the letter.

Step 3: Place the project on a shelf overnight to dry.

Activity #4: Track the Tree

Materials Needed:
- Outdoor Area near trees of any kind.
- One (1) piece of paper
- One (1) pen
- One (1) box of crayons

Instructions:

Step 1: Tell the child you're going to track some trees in the area.

Step 2: Take a walk around outside, near trees.

Step 3: While you're walking, have the child point to the trees. When they see a tree, have them use a pen to make a tally mark on the piece of paper.

Step 4: After the walk, ask the child to count the tally marks to find out how many trees they found.

Step 5: The adult should use a pen to write the number of trees next to the corresponding tally marks.

```
1 1 1 1 1 1 1    7 Trees
```

Step 6: Ask the child to use crayons to trace the number and then draw a picture of the trees they saw.

Step 7: Ask them the following questions:
- Were all of the trees the same or different?
- What makes them the same?
- What makes them different?
- Do you think you would see different trees in different parts of the world? Why?

Activity #5: Timer Turn

Materials Needed:
- A Timer (egg timer, timer on a cell phone or digital timer on an appliance)
- A space to move.

Instructions:

Step 1: Tell the child they're going to take turns dancing!

Step 2: Tell the child that you each are going to have thirty seconds to dance, and then it will be the other persons turn.

Step 3: Tell the child they will have the first turn. The adult should set the timer for thirty seconds.

Step 4: The adult should say, "Ready, Set, Go" then start the timer.

Step 5: When the timer beeps, the child should freeze.

Step 6: Now it's the adult's turn. Say, "Ready, Set, Go!" and the adult can dance for thirty seconds.

Step 7: When the timer beeps, the adult should freeze.

Step 8: Repeat step 3 through 7 at least 4 times.

Take it to the Next Level:

Continue the Timer Turn game with other objects or tasks. Some examples include:
- Bouncing a Ball
- Coloring on a piece of paper
- Building with blocks

Activity #1: "U"

Materials Needed:
- Paper
- Black Marker, Crayon or Pen
- Glue
- Crayons
- Yellow Highlighter

Instructions:

Step 1: The adult should draw a large "**U**" at the TOP of a piece of paper.

Step 2: Tell the child the "**U**" is **U**p at the top of the piece of paper.

Step 3: What object should go **U**nder the "**U**".

Step 4: Tell the child to use the yellow highlighter to trace the "**U**" at the top of the page.

Step 5: Ask the child use crayons to draw pictures of items under the "**U**".

Activity #2: Clay "U"

Materials Needed:
- Oven
- Clay Materials (see recipe)

Instructions:

Step 1: The adult and child should make Clay (see recipe at appendix A) together.

Step 2: Once made, roll the clay out into a long rope.

Step 3: Form the clay into the letter "**U**".

Step 4: Bake the clay as described in the recipe.

© JDEducational Curriculum Series: Level 2 Module 1

Activity #3: Clay "U" Decoration

Materials Needed:
- Baked "**U**" from Activity #2 (see above)
- Watercolors
- Optional: Sequins or glitter and glue

Instructions:

Step 1: Place the clay "**U**" on a baking tray lined with wax paper.

Step 2: Encourage the child to use watercolors and a paintbrush to paint the clay letter. If desired, provide the child with sequins or glitter and glue, allowing them to decorate the letter.

Step 3: Place the project on a shelf overnight to dry.

Activity #4: Under the Umbrella

Materials Needed:
- One (1) Umbrella
- One (1) Book: "Cloudy with a Chance of Meatballs" by Judi Barrett (if you can't make it to the library or own this book, please watch the story being read on the internet)
- One (1) Piece of Paper
- One (1) Box of Crayons

Instructions:

Step 1: Allow the child to sit outside **u**nderneath an open **u**mbrella.

Step 2: Read the story "Cloudy with a Chance of Meatballs" by Judi Barrett or watch someone read it on the Internet.

Step 3: Tell your child that you're going to make a menu together - something for breakfast, lunch and dinner. Maybe one day it will rain what they write down!

Step 4: Ask the child what they want it to rain for breakfast. Write down what they say on a blank piece of paper.

Step 5: Ask the child what they want it to rain for lunch. Write down what they say on the piece of paper.

Step 6: Ask the child what they want it to rain for dinner. Write down what they say on the piece of paper.

Step 7: Encourage the child to use crayons to draw pictures of the items on their menus.

Step 8: Ask the child what will help protect them when the food falls from the sky (Answer: stay **U**nder the **U**mbrella).

© JDEducational Curriculum Series: Level 2 Module 1

Activity #5: Upside-down Letter Detection.

Materials Needed:
- Twenty six (26) index cards (any color)
- One (1) Black Marker
- One (1) Table

Instructions:

Step 1: The adult should use a black marker to write each letter of the Alphabet (A through Z) on the index cards. They should write one letter on each index card.

Step 2: Tell the child you're going to play an Alphabet game. This game is called Upside-down Alphabet.

Step 3: Place two index cards in front of the child. One index card should have a letter that is right-side up, the other index card should have a letter that is upside down:

Step 4: Ask the child if they can tell you which letter is right-side up?

Step 5: Ask the child if they can tell you which letter is upside down?

Step 6: Were they right? Ask them to turn the upside-down letter right-side up.

Step 7: Next, ask the child to name each letter.

Step 8: Time to switch out the letters. The adult should place two new letters in front of the child.

Step 9: Repeat Step 3 through Step 8 at least 10 times.

Activity #1: Violet "V"

Materials Needed:
- One (1) Piece of Paper
- One (1) Black Marker
- One (1) Child-size art paint brush
- One (1) Tablespoon of Blue water based, non toxic paint
- One (1) Tablespoon of Red water based, non toxic paint
- One (1) Paper Bowl

Instructions:

Step 1: The adult should use a black marker to draw a "**V**" on a large piece of blank paper.

Step 2: The adult should ask the child to mix one tablespoon of blue paint and one tablespoon of red paint in a paper bowl.

Step 3: Encourage the child to use a paintbrush to paint the letter "**V**" with the new paint color. The color is called **V**iolet!

Activity #2: Clay "V"

Materials Needed:
- Oven
- Clay Materials (see recipe)

Instructions:

Step 1: The adult and child should make Clay (see recipe in Appendix A) together.

Step 2: Once made, roll the clay out into a long rope.

Step 3: Form the clay into the letter **"V"**.

Step 4: Bake the clay as described in the recipe.

© JDEducational Curriculum Series: Level 2 Module 1

Activity #3: Clay "V" Decoration

Materials Needed:
- Baked "**V**" from Activity #2 (see above)
- Watercolors
- Optional: Sequins or glitter and glue

Instructions:

Step 1: Place the clay "**V**" on a baking tray lined with wax paper.

Step 2: Encourage the child to use watercolors and a paintbrush to paint the clay letter. If desired, provide the child with sequins or glitter and glue, allowing them to decorate the letter.

Step 3: Place the project on a shelf overnight to dry.

Activity #4: The Vacation Planner

Materials Needed:
- One (1) box of Crayons
- One (1) Pen
- Two (2) Pieces of Paper

Instructions:

Step 1: Tell your child that you're going to create plans for your next family vacation.

Step 2: The adult should write "**Vacation**" on the top of the paper.

Step 3: Ask the child to tell you where they would like to go on **V**acation.

Step 4: The adult should write down what the child says.

Step 5: Next, ask the child to use crayons to draw a picture of the **V**acation on a of sheet blank paper.

© JDEducational Curriculum Series: Level 2 Module 1

Activity #5: Voice Volume

Materials Needed:
- One (1) area where noise won't disturb anyone around.

Instructions:

Step 1: Tell the child you're going to discover the "**V**olume of your **V**oices."

Step 2: Start with a **very quiet whisper v**oice and whisper:

"This is the very low **v**olume of our voice. This is the **v**olume we use when people are sleeping".

Ask the child to join you in the whisper **v**oice.

Step 3: Now raise your **v**oice **really, really loud** and say:

"This is the highest **v**olume of our **v**oice we use when there is danger and we need someone to hear us right away".

Have the child talk in their highest **v**olume **v**oice.

Step 4: Now speak in a regular tone and say:

"This is the **v**olume of our **v**oice we use when we're inside and when we're playing and laughing and talking to our friends and family".

Have the child practice talking in the inside **v**oice.

Step 5: Throughout the day, ask the child to give an example of each **v**olume of their **v**oice. Do they remember which **v**olume they are to use in different situations?

✏ Activity #1: Winter W

Materials Needed:
- One (1) Piece of paper
- One (1) Black Marker
- One (1) Cotton Ball
- Two (2) Tablespoons of White water-based, non-toxic paint

Instructions:

Step 1: The adult should draw a large "**W**" on a large piece of paper.

Step 2: Tell the child to paint the "**W**" **w**hite like **W**inter Snow.

Step 3: All the child to dip the cotton ball into the **W**hite paint and dab the "**W**" from Step 1 in **W**hite Snowballs.

✏ Activity #2: Clay "W"

Materials Needed:
- Oven
- Clay Materials (see recipe)

Instructions:

Step 1: The adult and child should make Clay (see recipe in Appendix A) together.

Step 2: Once made, roll the clay out into a long rope.

Step 3: Form the clay into the letter "**W**".

Step 4: Bake the clay as described in the recipe.

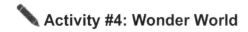 **Activity #3: Clay "W" Decoration**

Materials Needed:
- Baked "**W**" from Activity #2 (see above)
- Watercolors
- Optional: Sequins or glitter and glue

Instructions:

Step 1: Place the clay "**W**" on a baking tray lined with **w**ax paper.

Step 2: Encourage the child to use watercolors and a paintbrush to paint the clay letter. If desired, provide the child with sequins or glitter and glue, allowing them to decorate the letter.

Step 3: Place the project on a shelf overnight to dry.

 **Activity #4: Wonder World**

Materials Needed:
- A space near a Window in your home.
- Two (2) pieces of blank paper
- One (1) pen
- One (1) box of crayons

Instructions:

Step 1: The adult should use a pen to write the words "**W**onder **W**orld" on the top of one sheet of blank paper.

Step 2: Have the child sit near the **W**indow and ask them to look outside.

Step 3: The adult should tell the child that they are going to talk about the **W**orld outside.

Step 4: Using a pen, that adult should **w**rite down the child's answers to the following questions:

- o **W**hat is outside today?
- o **W**hat is happening outside today?
- o **W**hat questions to you have about **w**hat is outside today?
- o **W**hat do you **w**onder about the **w**orld?

Step 5: Ask the child to use crayons to draw a picture about the outside world on a blank piece of paper.

Step 6: Re-read what the child **w**rote about their **W**onder **W**orld from Step 4.

Activity #5: Wet Walk

Materials Needed:
- One (1) Bucket of Water that the child can step into.
- One (1) outside area with concrete
- One (1) Ruler
- One (1) Piece of Sidewalk Chalk

Instructions:

Step 1: The adult should place a bucket of water outside in an area that is surrounded by concrete.

Step 2: Tell the child to step into the bucket of water.

Step 3: Tell the child to step out of the bucket and take **four steps** on the concrete (help them count 1 through 4).

Step 4: After they're done making four footprints, help them us a ruler to measure each footprint.

Step 5: Using a piece of sidewalk chalk, write (in inches) how big each footprint is, next to each footprint.

Step 6: After measuring each footprint, ask the child if their footprints were all the same size. If not, ask them which one is the largest and which one is the smallest?

Step 7: Switch roles and have another child or the adult make new footprints.

Step 8: Repeat Step 4 and Step 5 with the new footprints.

Step 9: Compare everyone's footprints. Ask the child the following question:

- Whose footprints are larger?
- Whose footprints are smaller?

Step 10: Repeat step 3 through 8 and see if the footprints measured the same length again.

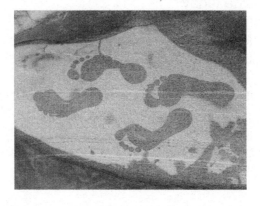

Activity #1: X

Materials Needed:
- One Piece of Paper
- One (1) Black Marker
- One (1) Bottle of Glitter
- One (1) Bottle of Elmer's Glue

Instructions:

Step 1: The adult should use a black marker to draw a large "**X**" on a large piece of blank paper.

Step 2: Allow the child to place Elmer's Glue on the "**X**". Help them if needed.

Step 3: Allow the child to use glitter to cover the "**X**".

Step 4: Place the "**X**" somewhere to dry.

Activity #2: Clay "X"

Materials Needed:
- Oven
- Clay Materials (see recipe)

Instructions:

Step 1: The adult and child should make Clay (see recipe in Appendix A) together.

Step 2: Once made, roll the clay out into a long line.

Step 3: Form the clay into the letter "**X**".

Step 4: Bake the clay as described in the recipe.

Activity #3: Clay "X" Decoration

Materials Needed:
- Baked "**X**" from Activity #2 (see above)
- Watercolors
- Optional: Sequins or glitter and glue

Instructions:

Step 1: Place the clay "**X**" on a baking tray lined with wax paper.

Step 2: Encourage the child to use watercolors and a paintbrush to paint the clay letter. If desired, provide the child with sequins or glitter and glue, allowing them to decorate the letter.

Step 3: Place the project on a shelf overnight to dry.

Activity #4: X Marks the Spot

Materials Needed:
- One (1) Large piece of paper
- One (1) Red Marker
- One (1) Piece of Yellow Construction Paper
- One (1) Pair of Adult Sized Scissors
- Five (5) 3x5 Cards
- One (1) Box of Crayons

Instructions:

Step 1: The adult should cut out ten small, round circles out of a yellow piece of construction paper. These "coins" will be the treasure.

Step 2: On the 3x5 cards, the adult should draw pictures of **five objects** in the home that the child can access. Each picture should be drawn on a separate 3x5 index card.

Step 3: The parent should hide two yellow coins next to each object they drew:

> **Example:** A photo of a toothbrush – the parent should place two coins next to their child's real toothbrush.

The pictures on the index cards will direct the child to the next object they need to find. These pictures are going to be clues to where the "**X**" (treasure) is hidden.

Place the index card with the "X" on it next to the last object the child will look for in the picture sequence (the last photo will be where X marks the spot). Place 10 more gold coins (pieces of paper) under the "X".

Step 4: Give the child the first clue index card and tell them to find that object.

Step 6: Once they find that object, they will use the picture next to that object to find the next object and "clue" index card.

Step 7: Help them along the way if they get frustrated. If they follow all of the pictures, it will lead them to the treasure at "**X**" marks the spot!

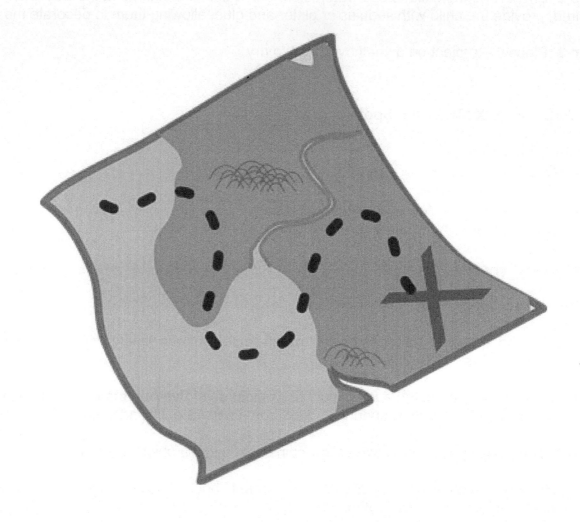

✏️ **Activity #1: Y**

Materials Needed:
- One Piece of Paper
- One (1) Black Marker
- One (1) Yellow Crayon

Instructions:

Step 1: The adult should use a black marker to draw a large "**Y**" on a large piece of blank paper.

Step 2: Allow your child to color the "**Y**" **Y**ellow.

Step 3: Ask the child to tell you what other things are **Y**ellow.

✏️ **Activity #2: Clay "**

Materials Needed:
- Oven
- Clay Materials (see recipe)

Instructions:

Step 1: The adult and child should make Clay (see recipe in Appendix A) together.

Step 2: Once made, roll the clay out into a long rope.

Step 3: Form the clay into the letter "**Y**".

Step 4: Bake the clay as described in the recipe.

Activity #3: Clay "Y" Decoration

Materials Needed:
- Baked "**Y**" from Activity #2 (see above)
- Watercolors
- Optional: Sequins or glitter and glue

Instructions:

Step 1: Place the clay "**Y**" on a baking tray lined with wax paper.

Step 2: Encourage the child to use watercolors and a paintbrush to paint the clay letter. If desired, provide the child with sequins or glitter and glue, allowing them to decorate the letter.

Step 3: Place the project on a shelf overnight to dry.

Activity #4: Yesterday, Today and Tomorrow

Materials Needed:
- One (1) Printed Calendar of the Month that is.
- One (1) Piece of Paper
- One (1) Box of Crayons

Instructions:

Step 1: Tell the child you're going to look at a calendar. Help them find today's date.

Step 2: Tell the child to draw a **green dot** in the box that is **"today"**.

Step 3: Tell the child you're going to find "**y**esterday". **Y**esterday is the day that came before today. Help show them the box on the calendar of the day before (**Y**esterday).

Step 4: Ask the child to write a "**Y**" in that box with a **Y**ellow crayon.

Step 5: Tell the child you're going to find "tomorrow". Tomorrow is the day after today. Show the child the box on the calendar of the day after today (Tomorrow).

Step 6: Ask them to write a "**T**" in that box with a **Blue crayon.**

Step 7: On a blank piece of paper, write down the child's answers to the following questions:

- What did we do **y**esterday (give them some clues if they can't remember)?
- What are we going to do today?
- What should we do tomorrow?

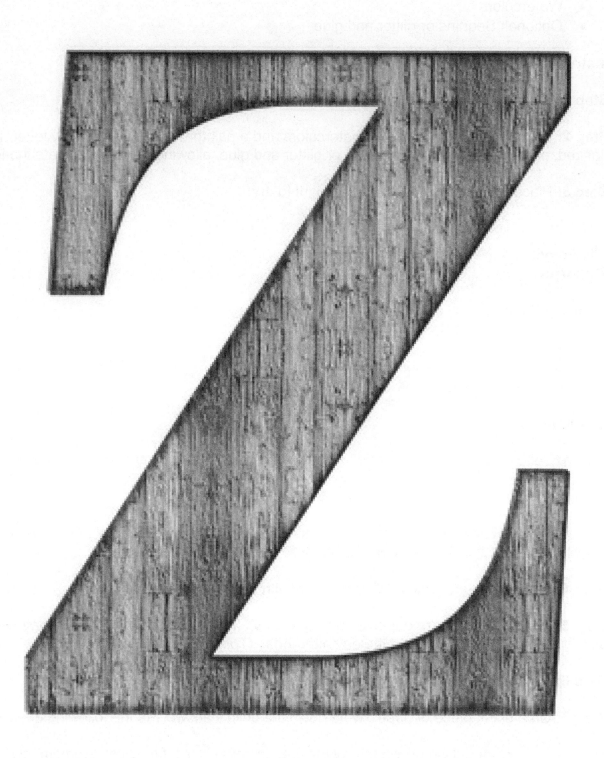

✏ Activity #1: Z

Materials Needed:
- One Piece of Paper
- One (1) Black Marker
- One (1) Bottle of Glitter
- One (1) Bottle of Elmer's Glue

Instructions:

Step 1: The child should use a black marker to draw a large **"Z"** on a large piece of blank paper.

Step 2: Allow the child to place Elmer's glue on the "**Z**". Help them if needed.

Step 3: Allow the child to cover the "**Z**" in glitter.

Step 4: Next, place the "**Z**" somewhere to dry.

✏ Activity #2: Clay "Z"

Materials Needed:
- Oven
- Clay Materials (see recipe)

Instructions:

Step 1: The adult and child should make Clay (see recipe in Appendix A) together.

Step 2: Once made, roll the clay out into a long rope

Step 3: Form the clay into the letter "**Z**".

Step 4: Bake the clay as described in the recipe.

Activity #3: Clay "Z" Decoration

Materials Needed:
- Baked "Z" from Activity #2 (see above)
- Watercolors
- Optional: Sequins or glitter and glue

Instructions:

Step 1: Place the clay "Z" on a baking tray lined with wax paper.

Step 2: Encourage the child to use watercolors and a paintbrush to paint the clay letter. If desired, provide the child with sequins or glitter and glue, allowing them to decorate the letter.

Step 3: Place the project on a shelf overnight to dry.

Activity #4: Zero

Materials Needed:
- Five (5) Small Crackers (Any kind)
- Five (5) Cheerios (Any Brand)
- Five (5) Small Banana Slices
- Five (5) Raisons
- One (1) Plate

Instructions:

Step 1: Tell the child you're going to practice counting backwards to the number **Z**ero.

Step 2: Place 5 small crackers on their plate. Ask them to count how many crackers there are (Answer: 1,2,3,4,5)

Step 3: Tell the child to eat one Cracker.

Step 4: Ask them to count how many crackers they have left (Answer: 1,2,3,4).

Step 5: Tell the child to eat one Cracker.

Step 6: Ask them to count how many crackers they have left (Answer: 1,2,3).

Step 7: Tell the child to eat one Cracker.

Step 8: Ask them to count how many crackers they have left (Answer: 1,2).

Step 9: Tell the child to eat one Cracker.

Step 10: Ask them to count how many crackers they have left (Answer: 1).

Step 11: Tell the child to eat one Cracker.

Step 12: Ask them to count how many crackers they have left (Answer: 0). They will most likely say "none" or "no more". Tell them there is a number for none. It is called "**Z**ero" it starts with a "**Z**".

Step 13: Repeat Steps 2 through 12 with the following:

- 5 cheerios
- 5 banana slices
- 5 raisons

Step 14: Continue practicing this at different meal times and snack times in order to begin practicing pre-subtraction/mathematical concepts.

ABC Review Game

Activity #1: ABC Review

Materials Needed:
- Twenty Six (26) Alphabet 3x5 index cards from Activity U-5 (Upside down Letters)
- One (1) Roll of painters tape.

Instructions:

Step 1: Place all 26 Alphabet 3x5 index cards on the floor. Place them into a large circle in order from A through Z. Make sure that each card **is at least 2 feet apart from each other**.

Step 2: The adult should use painters tape each card onto the floor to make sure the cards stay in one spot.

Step 3: Sing the "A B C" song with the child.

Step 4: Tell the child that they're going to play a hopping game.

Step 5: Have the child stand on letter "A" then **hop on one foot** to letter "B". Have the child shout out "letter B" when they hop on it.

Step 6: Tell the child to hop on one foot to the next letter. Ask them to shout out the name of each letter that they hop on. Continue until the child has named all the letters.

Take it to the Next Level:

The adult should mix the letters up and place them out of alphabetical order. Repeat Steps 2 through 6 and see if the child can name the letters they hop on when they are **out of order.**

(The adult can mix up the game by Jumping through the letters, skipping through the letters or running through the letters. Anything else?)

Appendix A:

Homemade Clay Recipe – For Activity 2 of All Letters of the Week Activities

> ** Note: This is a recipe I used for my preschool classes. You can search the internet for other recipes with variations.

Materials Needed
- ☐ 2 Cups Flour
- ☐ 2 Cups Salt
- ☐ 2 Tbsp Vegetable Oil
- ☐ 3/4 to 1 Cup Water

Directions:

Mix flour and salt together. Add oil and water. Stir mix until it becomes a smooth consistency.
Once completely mixed, make into desired shapes.
Bake clay shapes hard, bake in oven at 250 degrees for approximately 60 minutes.
Time may vary depending on how thick the clay is.

**Caution - Very thick clay shapes tend to crack when baked.

Pre-K Your Way Curriculum Series

© 2018 JDEducational
Curriculum Series materials may not be copied or distributed without written permission of
JD Educational. Additional curriculum can be purchased at www.jdeducational.com

About Our Curriculum

Our Curriculum is designed to strengthen school readiness by meeting the identified skills and concepts, which are necessary for a smooth transition to Kindergarten. These curriculum modules include low-cost/no-cost activities which parents, preschool staff and home daycare providers can use with the children in their care.

This curriculum was developed using current Kindergarten Readiness Assessments including: Common Core Kindergarten Standards, the Preschool Learning Foundation and the Desired Results Developmental Profile.

This curriculum addresses the following areas of development:

- Cognitive Development
- Mathematical Development
- Physical Development
- Language Development
- Literacy Development
- Social-Emotional Development
- Self-Help Skill Development

This curriculum was developed to meet the interests of all children and based on the multiple intelligences theory by Howard Gardner. Gardner was a Harvard University Professor who believed that traditional education wasn't utilizing the strengths of all children. Every child is unique and learns differently. Gardner identified eight different "intelligences" and pathways to learning.

These eight intelligences include:

1. Linguistic – "word smart"
2. Logical-Mathematical – "numbers/reasoning smart"
3. Spatial – "picture smart"
4. Bodily-Kinesthetic – "movement smart"
5. Musical – "Rhythms and songs smart"
6. Interpersonal – "People smart"
7. Intrapersonal – "Self smart"
8. Naturalist – "outdoors/nature smart"

About the Author: Jeana Kinne, MA

Kinne has worked in a variety of positions in the Early Childhood Education field. She received a Bachelor's degree in Sociology and Human Development, followed by a Master's degree in Education: Curriculum, Teaching and Learning with an emphasis in Child Psychology.

She has since held a variety of positions within the Child Development field – including Preschool Teacher/Director, Early Childhood Behavioral Specialist, Preschool Consultation Specialist, Parenting Educator and Early Intervention Specialist (working with infants and toddlers with developmental delays). She is also a guest lecturer at the local community college.

Through working with parents and other Early Childhood Professionals, it became clear that every child learns best through play, so she created the "Pre-K YOUR Way" Kindergarten Readiness Series.

Kinne, (along with her sweet golden retriever, Kona), created the *Sammy Series* and other JDEducational products, in order to encourage all children to love learning! More books from the *Sammy Book Series* are available at www.JDEducational.com and on Amazon.com.

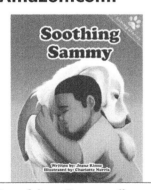

"Soothing Sammy" teaches children how to calm down, express their feelings and problem-solve in a positive way.

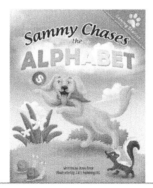

"Sammy Chases the Alphabet" teaches children letters and their sounds while Sammy plays fetch with letters.

"The Search for Sammy" teaches children how to stay safe if they get lost.

What's next? Pre-K YOUR Way Options:

There are includes 3 Levels. Each Level builds on concepts learned in the previous Level.

Level 1 Details:

Part 1: Themed Academic Activities which teach math, science, literacy, math and motor skills through a variety of 15 minute activities. There are 10 Activities for each of the following themes: All About Me, My Family, Emotions and Feelings, My 5 Senses, Nutrition, Mealtime, Literacy

Part 2: Everyday Learning Activities that teach academic skills. There are 10 Activities for each of the following: Going on a Walk, Taking Care of the Environment, Library Trips, Shopping, Riding in the Car, Playing at the Park and while at a Restaurant Games

Part 3: Behavior Support Tips & Reflections - Parenting Tip sections provide ideas and strategies to support age-appropriate social and emotional milestones (Including Understanding Diversity, Taking Turns with Loved Ones, Helping Parents Survive Restaurant Meals with Young Children and MORE!)

Your child is ready for this level if they can:

- Use words to communicate
- Follow Simple Directions
- Walk more than 5 steps
- Use a Crayon or Marker to draw
- Label familiar objects

Level 2: Details:

Each Unit includes 2 Parts:
Part 1: 90 Themed Academic Activities which use items found around the home to teach math, science, language, literacy, pre-writing skills. There are 15 Activities included in each theme. Themes include: My Community, Roadways and Signs, Advanced Opposites, Space Exploration, Investigating My Home and Advanced Numbers, Letters and Shapes.

Your child is ready for this level if they can:

- Complete 2-part patterns
- Name familiar shapes
- Count 5 objects
- Identify colors
- Follow directions
- Imitate lines with a marker or crayon.

Level 3: Details:

Part 1: 90 Themed Academic Activities which use items found around the home to teach math, science, language, literacy, pre-writing skills. Themes include: Camping, Transportation, Planet Earth, Construction, Oceanography and Weather!

Part 2: 6 Multi-Step Projects. These projects teach children how academic skills are used in the real world. Projects include: Project Transportation: Understanding Package Delivery Systems; Project Weather: Discovering the Elements; Project Earth: Investigating Earths Layers - Reduce, Reuse and Recycle; Project Construction: Building Components and Design and Project Ocean: Oceanography - Introduction to Photosynthesis.

<u>Your child is ready for this level if they can:</u>

- Recite numbers 1 through 10 in order
- Describe similarities and differences of several shapes
- Retell a story
- Write all uppercase letters of the Alphabet and recognize their sounds.
- Follow two-step directions
- Use child-sized scissors

Visit www.jdeducational.com for more information!

Level 3: Details.

Part 1: Themed Academic Activities which use items found around the home to teach math, science and upper literacy/prewriting skills. Themes include: Camping, Transportation, Planet Earth, Color Theme, Oceanography, and Weather.

Part 2: 5 Life skill Projects: These projects teach children how academic skills are used in the real world. Projects include: Project T (shape art for measuring), Package Delivery Service, Project Weather (Tissor and the Elements, Jr. mechanics), Investigating Baths, Layers, Reduce, Reuse, and Recycle Project, Orientation, Building Components, and Design Project Closer, Oceanography, Introduction to Photosynthesis.

Your child is ready for this level if they can:

- Recite numbers 1 through 10 in order.
- Describe similarities and differences of several shapes.
- Recite a story.
- Write all upper case letters OR children that recognize their sounds.
- Draw simple pictograms.
- Speak in clear sentences.

Made in the USA
Monee, IL
01 October 2020